About the Author

Mildred Tengbom is a dedicated Christian servant who has
served as a missionary in India and, together with her husband, Luverne, in Tanzania and Singapore. Drawing on her
lifelong Bible study and rich experience as a missionary, wife,
and mother, she has published many articles and stories and
more than 15 books, including *Bible Readings for Families*,
Table Prayers, *Mealtime Prayers*, and *Why Waste Your Illness?*
The Tengboms now make their home in California.

Bible Readings for

Mothers

Bible Readings for

Mothers

Mildred Tengbom

Augsburg
MINNEAPOLIS

To J., J., and B.

BIBLE READINGS FOR MOTHERS

1996 edition

Copyright © 1996 Augsburg Fortress. All rights reserved. Except for brief quotations in critical articles or reviews, no part of this book may be reproduced in any manner without prior written permission from the publisher. Write to: Permissions, Augsburg Fortress, 426 S. Fifth St., Box 1209, Minneapolis MN 55440.

Scripture quotations unless otherwise noted are from the Holy Bible: New International Version. Copyright 1973, 1978, 1984 by the International Bible Society. Used by permission of Zondervan Bible Publishers.

Back cover scripture quotation is from the New Revised Standard Version Bible, copyright © 1989 by the Division of Christian Education of the National Council of the Churches of Christ in the USA and used by permission.

The Library of Congress has cataloged the 1987 edition as follows:

Tengbom, Mildred.
   Bible readings for mothers.
     1. Mothers—Prayer-books and devotions—English.
I. Title.
BV4847.T46   1987   242'.6431   87-1051
ISBN 0-8066-2249-0

ISBN 0-8066-2988-6 (1996 edition)

The paper used in this publication meets the minimum requirements of American National Standard for Information Sciences—Permanence of Paper for Printed Library Materials, ANSI Z329.48-1984.   ∞

Manufactured in the U.S.A.   AF 9-2988

00   99   98   97   96   1   2   3   4   5   6   7   8   9   10

Giving Birth to New Life

"A woman giving birth has pain . . . but when her baby is born she forgets the anguish because of her joy that a child is born" (John 16:21).

Expectant mothers prepare for the discomfort, labor, and pain of giving birth by learning certain techniques to distract their attention from the pain.

Even then, though many mothers give birth comparatively easily (is any birthing easy?), some mothers suffer greatly. When the latter happens, the mother may be so exhausted and sore she may feel more relief than joy when her baby finally is born. She may need to sleep, rest, and recover before she experiences joy rippling through her as she holds in her arms her baby—*her* baby whom she carried for so many months within the coziness and warmth of her own body. Gazing into the face of her little one now she sees also a mysterious little stranger who has come to live with her. Then it is that joy replaces pain and wonder replaces weariness.

Jesus compared the pain his disciples would experience when he died to the pain of giving birth. "You will grieve and lament, but I promise you," he said, referring to his resurrection that would follow, "joy will replace your pain."

Again and again in life we suffer little "labor pains" to give birth to new life. The important thing is to learn how to bear the pain so the new life can emerge. Jesus stands ready to help us if we only ask him to help. And it is he who gives us new life beyond the pain.

> Oh, God, give us a faith that in all situations can lean upon you and trust you even as a helpless babe trusts the mother.

Quietly review some hard times you have known. What treasures have you been able to extract from them?

7

Sturdy Love

"And a sword will pierce your own soul too" (Luke 2:35).

In that cowshed in Bethlehem long ago, how could Mary have envisioned what life would hold for her? In the years that followed, her love for God and her child led her to experiences that were sometimes astonishing and animating, sometimes puzzling and perplexing, sometimes disquieting and disturbing, sometimes pulverizing and prostrating, and then finally, at Easter, electrifying and ecstatic.

How true for us as mothers, too! At the radiant moment of birth few anxious thoughts about the future flit through our minds. The joy and exaltation of the present moment capture us entirely. Perhaps just as well. Best to take one day and one experience at a time.

However, let us pray for a faith to trust God to keep our children true to him in spite of all we shall fail to do or be, and for a faith to continue trusting him when bad things happen to our children. Let us pray also that our love for them shall remain constant even if they hurt us, switch us off when we warn them of danger, or make decisions contrary to our better judgment.

Oh, God, I believe you are able to do far above all I ask or think. Help my unbelief.

Have you ever regretted having children? Talk to Jesus about those experiences that have been painful.

Life is Never the Same after the Firstborn

"She gave birth to her firstborn, a son" (Luke 2:7).

Becoming a mother ushered in for Mary a never-ending succession of joys and sorrow, anxieties and hopes, dreams and disappointments, pride and shame, vitality and weariness. She became a refugee and later, perhaps, a single parent, since scholars believe she was widowed early. Everything about Mary's life changed.

A mother spends her whole lifetime learning all that is involved in being a mother. A wife's relationship with her husband changes. Tensions develop as parents face sleeplessness punctuated with crying children, anxious times of illness, and sometimes conflict and disagreement in regard to discipline. Many mothers are wage earners outside the home. In a single parent family the mother may have responsibility for emotional, disciplinary, and financial support. Some mothers have to assume responsibility in caring for aging parents, or welcome home again grown children, or nurture growing grandchildren.

If at the beginning we could have grasped the immensity and difficulty of our task, would we ever have had the courage to have taken that first step?

> O living Christ, thank you for the privilege and honor
> of being a mother. Where I have failed, forgive. Give
> me the strength, love, and patience that I lack.

Spend a few moments thanking God for all the good things being a mother has brought you.

Plans that Were Upset

"She went home and found her child lying on the bed, and the demon gone" (Mark 7:30).

Jesus wanted to get away to have some undisturbed time with his disciples. Perhaps he wanted to prepare them for the dark days looming ahead when he would be captured, tried, and killed, when they would be thrown into confusion and doubt. So, taking his disciples with him, he set off for what today we know as Lebanon. He entered a house "and did not want anyone to know it." Yet a woman whose child was tortured by a demon insisted Jesus help her. "Send her away," the disciples said. She was spoiling their retreat, interfering with their time off.

Jesus met this interruption the way he always did: he put aside his own interests, recognized the woman's need and faith, and pronounced healing for her child. He turned the intrusion into an opportunity for selfless service.

Can we, like Jesus, embrace interruptions as opportunities to "count others better than ourselves," to "deny ourselves," to seek the good of others? Difficult, demanding words, but it is the way Jesus went, and he calls us to follow him.

O God, I confess I do not find it easy to put self-interests aside. Help me to allow you to live out your life through me.

Next time an interruption upsets and annoys you, stop and ask God, "What are you trying to say to me?"

Out of the Mouths of Babes

"Have you never read, 'from the lips of children and infants you have ordained praise'?" (Matthew 21:16).

One of the great joys of new motherhood is watching your child grow and learn. It is amazing how quickly a baby changes and develops.

Perhaps even more exciting is the time when your child first learns to speak. Within a few short years, children are able to master most of the basics of language—and they do it almost entirely by imitation.

God has given children the exceptional gifts of observation. Very quickly, they pick up the phrases and behavior of the adults and others around them. Parents are often startled what comes out of their children's mouths.

Jesus knew the capacities of children for observing their world and seeing things just as they are. Unlike adults, young children have not yet learned to hide what they know to be the truth, and they are not as inclined toward self-deception.

It is no wonder that Jesus enjoyed children and talked about the importance of a childlike faith. Each of us can learn about openness to God from watching the way children respond.

> Dear God, give me the eyes of a child to see your Son
> and the truth more clearly.

What are the biggest influences on your children right now? Can they be improved?

What We Gain from Listening

"She had a sister called Mary, who sat at the Lord's feet listening to what he said" (Luke 10:39).

Bethany, where Mary, Martha, and Lazarus lived, was two miles from Jerusalem. Jesus liked to drop in and stay there. The four were good friends.

Not that the three could always understand their friend. Sometimes he was unpredictable, as when he delayed coming when Lazarus was ill. The sisters also felt uneasy because Jesus talked so much about dying. He was too young to do that!

So one day when Jesus arrived, Mary sat down next to him and began to listen. The subject of their conversation is not given. But with Jesus' death so imminent, perhaps, among other things, he spoke about what he expected would happen in the days to come. Did he also try to enlighten Mary as to who he was? In Greek the word for *listen* has more the complete meaning of "learning something about someone."

Gathering all the information we can is the first step in dealing with anxiety. At the same time we need to accompany this with learning more about our Lord—who he is, his love, and his power. Mary acted wisely by taking the time to do both.

> *We long to see the footprints where you, O Jesus, have trod, to know you have gone before us and will lead our way to God.*

What are you doing to build up your faith in God?

I'm So Tired!

"Those who hope in the Lord will renew their strength" (Isaiah 40:31).

A teething baby, an into-everything three-year-old, and a guest had left the young mother in tears. "I'm so tired!" she sobbed into her husband's shoulder. "Sometimes I feel as though I've been tired for a hundred years."

Here's how Beverly Jones expressed this truth: "The most automated appliance in a household is the mother." The difference is mothers get tired when appliances don't.

The Mayo Clinic identified four basic needs that must be kept in balance to avoid exhaustion. Using the four components in Dr. Richard Clark Cabot's formula for life—work, play, love, and worship—a symbol with four arms of equal length was developed. Whenever one or more of those arms becomes shortened, the person feels unhappy, and unhappiness often precipitates tiredness.

Many mothers complain of chronic tiredness. A mother's arms may be long on work and love, but short on worship or play. Her children's arms might be long on play and love—and maybe even worship—but short on work.

If you feel like you've been tired all your life, take a look at your four arms. Are all of equal length?

O Christ, the daily contact with life and people wears and tears at me. Teach me how to find renewal.

Decide what you can do to bring better balance between your four arms of work, play, love, and worship.

The Importance of Touch

"People were also bringing babies to Jesus to have him touch them" (Luke 18:15).

Jesus understood the importance of expressing love by touching. He took time to pick up the children, to hold them in his arms, to lay his hands in blessing on their heads as he prayed for them.

While living in Nepal, I observed a lovely custom. Every morning and evening the children stand before their parents with bowed heads, waiting for the parents to lay hands on their heads and bless them. This gesture on the part of the parents indicates acceptance, approval, and wishes for the well-being of the child.

George Eliot once expressed the opinion that in the person "whose childhood has known caresses there lies a fibre of memory which can be touched to noble issues."

Holding, caressing, and touching a child can convey assurance of love and acceptance. With that assurance comes a feeling of security and wholeness that frees a person to reach out. When we know we are loved, it is easy to love others and respond to the needs of others.

> Thank you, Jesus, that I have felt your touch on my life. Thank you for all who have embraced me, held me in their arms, loved, and comforted me. Remind me to use this expression of love wisely and often.

Can you remember times when somebody's embrace had special significance and comfort for you? How do you express love to the members of your family?

Lasting Influences

"Train a child in the way he should not go, and when he is old he will not turn from it" (Proverbs 22:6).

By the time our children reach the teenage years—that exciting and dangerous time of testing their own judgment—we have already done most of what we can do to prepare them for adult life. Psychologists tell us that the basic personalities and behavioral patterns of our children are well established within the first three to five years of life.

The time that we spend with our children as new parents is extremely formative. The holding, cuddling, smiling, and talking develop a relationship of trust and a sense of security from the very beginning.

Sometimes parents take their responsibilities so seriously that they become anxious about every little detail. That is when it is important to realize that, as important as we are to our children, they are new creations of God with their own wills and their own choices to make. We can give them the love and security that they need to adjust to life, but we cannot ultimately control them. We can help them grow as best as we know how, and then we trust them to God.

> *Dear God, being a parent is exciting and frightening at the same time. Give me wisdom and a sense of trust in you, and reassure me of your care and forgiveness when I make mistakes.*

Is there a parent support group in your church or community that you could join?

Worries, Worries, Worries

"But seek his kingdom, and these things will be given to you as well" (Luke 12:31).

All of us mothers know anxieties: young mothers establishing homes, single mothers supporting families, mothers helping to pay tuition costs and caring for aged parents, mothers who are widows living on fixed incomes and watching the rents rise and the tally on grocery bills growing even higher.

When Jesus spoke these words about our needs being provided, he was not a millionaire telling the unemployed that the papers were full of help-wanted ads. Having grown up in a poor home, and quite likely having had to provide for his widowed mother and his younger brothers and sisters, Jesus knew about needs firsthand. But he was also sure that his Father would provide.

If we, as best we can with our human limitations, seek God's will first, we can turn to him and say, "I have this new need, Father. You have promised. I trust you to supply." Over and over it has been my unfailing experience to witness God meeting our needs. He is trustworthy. We praise and thank him.

> God, we thank you that we can bring large petitions to you, knowing that your grace and power are such we can never ask you too much.

Recall some of the times God met your needs.

But What Will Happen to You?

"At this they wept again. Then Orpah kissed her mother-in-law goodbye, but Ruth clung to her" (Ruth 1:14).

The book of Ruth portrays many warm relationships of loving and caring within a family. We see it first in Naomi's concern for the future of her two daughters-in-law. With her husband and both sons dead, Naomi could have begged Ruth and Orpah to stay with her. Instead, Naomi thought not of herself, but of the young widows and what would be best for them. They were still young. If they returned to their own people, she said, they stood good chances of remarrying.

Ruth, however, also refused to think of herself. She loved Naomi and could not bear the thought of leaving her on her own. Even if it meant continuing to live away from her own extended family, Ruth was prepared for this.

One of the ingredients of a happy family life is so simple that we stumble and miss it. What is it? Unselfishness. That is, each member asks himself or herself, "What can I do to make life easier and more pleasant for my husband, my wife, my children, my in-laws, my aging parents?" When this attitude prevails, no one loses; everyone gains. It's worth a try!

Loving God, help me always to remember my Savior's eagerness, not to be waited upon, but to serve. Enable our family to discover this joyous and noble way of life.

How can this principle be helpful in your family?

The Gift of Graciousness

"Now Naomi had a relative on her husband's side…
whose name was Boaz" (Ruth 21:1).

Skillfully the writer of the book of Ruth sketches the character of Boaz by showing us through Boaz's actions what kind of a person he was. Boaz greeted his workers with, "The Lord be with you!" (v.4). A genial, harmonious relationship must have existed between employer and employees, for they responded with, "The Lord bless you!"

Boaz inquired about Ruth, then displayed the utmost courtesy toward her. He invited her to continue to glean in his fields. Concerned for her safety, he urged her to stay close to his servant girls and promised her protection from the men. He invited her to drink water freely from the jugs his men had brought. He praised her for her kindness to Naomi. He prayed God's blessing on her life. At noon he invited her to lunch. He told the harvesters to pull out some of the full stalks of wheat and leave them for her.

Joseph Joubert said that Boaz "wore his velvet within"—that is, he showed himself most amiable, most courteous, and most gracious to those of his own house. Saying "please," "thank you," "I appreciate . . . ," "You did a great job!" create enriched, happier relationships in the home along with the smiles which accompany any help we give others.

> Forgive me, gracious God, when hurried and worried I
> forget to be thoughtful, kind, courteous, or gracious to
> me family.

Family life embraces little rituals. Can you think of some small way you can express courtesy to your family daily?

How to Influence People

"Then Ruth told her mother-in-law about the one at whose place she had been working" (Ruth 2:19).

When Boaz first addressed Ruth as "my daughter," Ruth must have been set at ease immediately, even though she undoubtedly was surprised. She responded by bowing her face to the ground in respect. Boaz's kindness humbled her, as kindness always does. Later she told Boaz he had given her comfort and spoken kindly to her, even though she felt she hadn't deserved it.

After she got home, she still marveled over what had happened. She told Naomi about the events of the day: "He even said to me, 'Stay with my workers until they finish harvesting all my grain'" (v.21).

Naomi was thrilled. She saw not only Boaz's kindness, but behind that a God who remembered them and their needs.

Through our courtesy, kindness, and generosity our children and others too can be introduced to God.

Gracious God, such wonderful things happen in the hearts of people when they are shown courtesy, kindness, and generosity. Teach me to be more thoughtful so I may recognize opportunities to show your love.

How would concentration on developing these qualities affect the atmosphere of your home and your ministry?

Run Your Race to Win

"Run in such a way as to get the prize" (1 Corinthians 9:24).

No one had ever told me how terribly difficult it would be to blend two families," a young divorced mother who had remarried said. "If I had known, I don't think I would have dared to try."

Blended families, even more than other families, need to be realistic in their expectations. They shouldn't expect that everybody will like everybody instantly.

Parents especially need to be understanding of the children suddenly brought together under one roof. Don't expect them to be "milers" in their achievements.

Decide at the beginning that you are going to make a go of it. Determine that you will try your best. Declare it to yourself every morning. Let your children know that you intend to succeed. With this perspective, you won't be overwhelmed by quarrels, misunderstandings, bitter words, and disagreements because you will be able to see them as temporary roadblocks. Obstacles will be cleared out, as your goal remains unchanged.

> O God, you have pity on your stumbling, weak children, give us an endurance charged with a faith that believes what we are looking for and praying for will indeed come to pass.

How can determining to succeed alleviate anxiety?

Winter's Special Gift

"And this is my prayer: that your love may abound more and more in knowledge and depth of insight, so that you may be able to discern what is best" (Philippians 1:9).

I stood with my 84-year-old mother, looking out at the snow falling gently outside, clothing the world in white. A blue jay and a cardinal fluttering around mother's bird feeder, scolding each other, caught our attention. They were vying for the grain we had put out for them.

How vivid their color's are!" I cried. "The red, the blue, the black. Do their colors actually get deeper in the winter?"

My gray-haired mother smiled knowingly. "No," she said. "It's just that in winter when everything gets covered with snow, we see less and so we see better."

Wintry times of trouble, disappointment, sickness, and suffering can so dominate our lives that they block out many things that used to concern us.

Nancy Reagan, writing about her husband, President Ronald Reagan, said Alzheimer's disease is taking a toll on him and on the family, and she noted, "Illness brings things into focus and should reshuffle our priorities."

Paul's prayer for his friends in Philippi was that they would be able to see things more clearly through their suffering so they could discern, not only what is good, but what is *best*.

> *What things am I not seeing clearly, dear Lord? Am I missing the mark in the way I am living? If so, correct my vision.*

Can you recall troubled times when you began to look differently at life? What things became unimportant? Important? Have you let that insight continue to guide you?

How Do You Handle Anxieties?

"They . . . were afraid to ask" (Mark 9:32).

A woman may procrastinate in going to the doctor about the lump in her breast because she's afraid the doctor may tell her what she doesn't want to hear.

Jesus' friends didn't like the way kept on talking about dying. He was only 33! What did he mean? They wanted to ask, but they didn't dare. They were afraid to hear what he might say. Yet not knowing made them irritable, so they began to bicker among themselves: "I'm better than you." "No, I am!"

Jesus took a child and put him in their midst. "Swallow your pride and become like a child," he said. What a strange thing to say when they were already acting childish by quarreling about who was the greatest. But, at the same time, they were not acting like children, because they were afraid to ask questions, and we know that asking questions is one thing children aren't afraid to do.

Do we dare to voice our anxieties, or do we try to smother them? Smothering anxieties may result in eruption of arguing, bickering, and picking on one another. Feelings of guilt follow. What a miserable way to handle our worries! If we have questions, let's ask them. They can alleviate anxiety and also show us what to do. Questions are a much better way to handle worries.

Give us wisdom and courage to face life realistically.

What questions have you been afraid to ask?

Don't Panic

"It is not good to have zeal without knowledge, nor to be hasty and miss the way" (Proverbs 19:2).

Years ago I was on a train in Pakistan, headed for the Northwest Frontier Region, an area known for brigands and violence. As a young girl traveling alone, I began to feel jittery. Then I had to go to the restroom. As I was cooped up in the tiny, smelly enclosure, the lights went out and I was plunged into darkness. *Someone's turned of the lights on purpose,* I thought, and grabbed the door handle and pushed. The door didn't budge. I pushed harder. Still it didn't move. *They've blocked the door and probably are going through my luggage,* I thought. I pounded on the door. No response. I leaned against what I thought was the wall, but proved to be the door, for it shot open and I fell into the coach. My luggage was intact; my fears had been groundless. What I had thought to be the handle of the door was the empty towel rack on the wall.

When events plunge us into confusion and we panic, we're apt to get ensnarled with needless, groundless worries and fears. When pressure builds, send up a prayer for calmness and guidance. Wait until your heart is calm. Then you will be able to think clearly enough to understand your situation and make wise decisions.

> *Teach me not to panic, O God, when scary situations throw me into confusion. Help me to remember you are with me and will guide me.*

What situations still upset you? What can you do to handle them better?

Jesus Can Heal

" 'Neither this man nor his parents sinned,' said Jesus, 'but this happened so that the work of God might be displayed in his life' " (John 9:3).

Is the baby all right?" If the words are not actually uttered, they are on the edge of a mother's thoughts as she carefully examines her newborn child. If something is not normal, most mothers struggle with feelings of inadequacy, failure, and maybe even guilt.

All three feelings tortured me when our first two sons, born prematurely, died within a few hours of their births. I felt guilty, because I wondered if I had been careful enough. I felt failure, because I had not succeeded in carrying them full term—and it happened twice. I felt like an inadequate mother, because I had not been able to shelter my babies within my body until they were mature enough to make it on their own.

The pain associated with these feelings is intense and longer lasting and more difficult to relieve than any physical pains of childbirth. Only Jesus can heal these emotional wounds. He assures us that he is not punishing us, but that, turned over to him, even this sorrow can become a means of bringing glory to God.

O Christ, our Redeemer, set me free from feelings of inadequacy, failure, and guilt that cripple me. Help me focus instead on all that I have in you.

Talk to Jesus about any feelings of failure, inadequacy, or guilt that trouble you. Accept the reassurance and encouragement God offers you.

Pulling Together

"There [Paul] met a Jew named Aquila . . . with his wife Priscilla" (Acts 18:2).

Some years ago when we visited the Vellore Christian Medical Center in India, we met two young doctors working side by side. Mark, an American, was a staff physician and engaged also in research. Elisabeth, a Norwegian, was working in public health. These two, who had joined their lives in marriage, not only shared common careers but they were working together in teaching Bible classes to medical students and in seeking to impart Christian values to their three children.

Mark and Elisabeth are among those who have followed in the footsteps of Priscilla and Aquila, the first Christian couple mentioned by name in the New Testament as sharing a common trade—tentmaking. When they heard Christ's call to follow him they continued their tentmaking but also found ways to work in the Christian community.

For Priscilla and Elisabeth and for many Christian mothers today, responsibilities include working outside the home, earning a living, nurturing and caring for their children, and in addition, finding ways to reach out in Christian service.

Help me understand, O God, how you want me to serve you.

What difference does it make when we can see our daily tasks as our service to God?

A Pine Tree Instead of a Thornbush

"Instead of the thornbush will grow the pine tree, and instead of briers the myrtle will grow" (Isaiah 55:13).

She sat, face buried in her hands, sobbing. Broken words poured out. "Our family—always respected. Such godly heritage all of our kids have had! We've cherished such great dreams for them. And now, Linda an unwed mother. Joel an alcoholic—at 22!" There was silence for a while, except for sobbing, then, "Our family is finished."

"I don't think so," her friend said. "You may have to relinquish some dreams you cherished for your children. maybe they won't succeed in the way that you had hoped they would. Perhaps that's not important just now. But you can still hope for the truly important goals of life for them: rehabilitation, restoration, a realization of their need for God, and a turning to him."

The Bible is honest in describing the weaknesses of people, but it also shows there is always hope for change. David committed adultery and murder, but repented and was restored. Moses ran away from God but came back.

God is a Savior. Even if fond dreams we have had for our young people crumble, we need not abandon hope. God is still able to save them.

Savior God, I walk steadier when I recall that though we slip, you do not fall.

When you pray for your loved ones who have slipped, visualize them as changed people, in love with God.

Hanging In

"When Jesus saw their faith, he said to the paralytic, 'Son, your sins are forgiven'" (Mark 2:5).

The four friends were determined to get their paralyzed friend to Jesus. When they couldn't get near the door, they removed the roof tiles and lowered their friend's pallet into the room where Jesus was. What a sight that must have been! Can't you see Jesus' look of astonishment and delight?

Faith is hanging in there. Abraham hung in until he was almost a hundred before his son was born. Hannah kept on praying for a child year after year. Joseph was so sure his grandchildren or great-grandchildren would get back to his homeland that he told them not to forget to take his bones with them when they went.

Has God given you some promise that you haven't seen fulfilled yet? Are you still struggling to overcome some bad habit? Have your children strayed from the Lord? Do your parents not yet confess Christ as their Savior? Don't give up. When Jesus saw the faith of the four men, he forgave and healed the paralytic. The Lord loves to find faith. If your loved ones can't believe, exercise faith on their behalf. Jesus will be glorified as people give their hearts to him.

O God of all hopefulness, help us to always persevere in believing.

Thank God that he is working in the hearts of those you love.

When Doubts Come

"Then he said to Thomas, 'Put your finger here. . . . Stop doubting and believe'" (John 20:27).

Doubts about God were torturing my friend who was going through a long period of illness. One day he said to me, "The doctrine of the Trinity makes no sense to me. If I can't figure out how it all hangs together, I can't believe."

A bouquet of daisies sat on the table by his bed. I picked one and ripped off the petals one by one until only the naked stem was left.

"Why did you do that?" my friend cried. "All the beauty is gone!"

"Following and loving God requires faith," I said gently. "I can't understand everything about God, but I can believe in him. When I try to understand God, it's like ripping the petals off this flowers. When I do this, what is left?"

My friend stared.

"A man who suffered much," I continued, "once said that to stand on one leg and prove God's existence is a very different thing from going down on one's knees and thanking him."

> Almighty and eternal God, hidden from my sight, infinite beyond the comprehension of my limited mind, whose ways are often indiscernible and mysterious, and whose thoughts are vastly different from my thoughts, I worship you.

If you are struggling with doubts, try worshiping God.

How Can I Manage My Time Wisely?

"But seek first his kingdom and his righteousness, and all these things will be given you as well" (Matthew 6:33).

In an interview, Dan Rather told of how Eric Sevareid had warned him that as a TV anchorman, stationed in one place, he would be a target for people who would be time wasters. To help discipline himself, Rather wrote on three pieces of paper the question: "Is what you're doing now helping the broadcast?" He put one slip in his billfold, one in his pocket, and one on his desk. From time to time he looks at them.

Maybe we need to write and post pieces of paper on which we would ask, "Is what I am doing now helping me seek the kingdom of God and his righteousness?"

> *Gracious God, giver of life and health, of opportunities and time, help me remember that today well lived will make every yesterday a memory of happiness and every tomorrow a vision of hope. Help me, therefore, look well to this day and live it seeking to know you better and to walk in a way that will bring joy to you.*

Would the way you spend your time change if you posted and heeded this question: "Is the way I am spending my time helping me obey Jesus' command to seek first the kingdom of God?" In what ways would it change?

Sing Your Fears Away

"Paul and Silas were praying and singing hymns to God" (Acts 16:25).

Paul and Silas had been beaten and tossed into jail. How were they feeling besides hurting from their sore backs? Weren't they afraid? My guess is they were. How could they know what kind of treatment they would get the next morning? Or what would happen to them in the future? To fear is to be human. Why were they singing? Did they hurt so much they couldn't sleep and so were trying to distract their attention from their pain? Did they find that singing helped them feel less afraid, too?

When my friend Bob Lange was slowly dying of Lou Gehrig's disease, he said to me, "Whenever I start to think of the future and become afraid, I call Maggie [his wife] to come. I ask her to sit at the piano and play. Then we sing and sing together until we have sung my fears away." That's facing a threatening future with courage.

Do you ever become afraid? Sometimes when I listen to stories of violence and turbulence, I can feel fear creeping in, wondering what the future will hold for our children and grandchildren. I get scared, too, when a loved one becomes seriously ill. Then I try to remember Bob's example. I'm not a soloist—I'm not even a choir member—but I sing and sing until I've sung the gloomies out of my heart and home. Maybe you would like to try singing the next time you become afraid.

Lord Jesus, make yourself an evermore present reality to me. Thank you for the gift of song. Thank you for helping me when I become afraid.

When you talk to your children about being afraid, what do they mention? How do you help them with their fears?

The Loss of Innocence

"I tell you the truth, unless you change and become like children, you will never enter the kingdom of heaven" (Matthew 18:3).

I finished reading our little daughter a fairy tale with a happy ending—so pleasing, so right, so perfect. With a sigh she asked, "Is it true?" Already, young as she was, she was beginning to struggle with the hard facts of our often cruel world. At the time she was sick with an illness that was evading diagnosis. Her little brother's dearly loved African playmate had died. And when she was 300 miles away at boarding school, she was often homesick. Small wonder she asked about the story with the happy ending: "Is it true?" Already our broken world was becoming more real than the happy world of fairy tales.

At times like this we must guide our children gently and wisely so cynicism will not conquer trust, and doubt will not replace faith. Our goal is to share our sure conviction that God will always walk with them—even at times they may not be conscious of his presence—and that in the end he can bring good out of everything—even though it may not seem possible at the time.

Dear God, help me through those difficult times when it's hard to believe you can work out things for me and those I love.

What are you doing to nurture your children's faith in God?

Getting Along with Difficult People

"Live in harmony with one another" (Romans 12:16).

My mother-in-law is impossible to live with," a young woman complained. "No one can please her. What can a person do to get along with such an impossible woman?"

Paul had some succinct advice to give in Romans 12.

1. "Love must be sincere. Hate what is evil; cling to what is good." You don't have to *like* the un-Christlike qualities you see in her, but she must have some good points. Focus on those.

2. "Be devoted to one another in brotherly [sisterly] love." To love different from liking. One can *will* to love. And if you will to love, you can accompany it with some show of affection—if the other person allows it—without feeling like a hypocrite.

3. "Honor one another above yourselves." Think of every way you can to show respect and honor. Your tone of voice. The terms by which you address her. Can you open doors for her? Show courtesy?

If this seems wearying, remember Paul added: "Never be lacking in zeal, but keep your spiritual fervor." Stay so in love with Jesus that even living with an impossible woman becomes possible. Your service to her is service to the Lord.

O God, help me do what I myself cannot do.

Think of a difficult person in your life. How would you apply Paul's advice to this relationship?

Pray for that Difficult Person

"Be . . . faithful in prayer" (Romans 12:12).

Paul continues with words of wisdom on how to live with difficult people:

1. "Be joyful in hope." When you pray, visualize this person changed. Thank God it will be so.

2. "Share with God's people who are in need." Ask God to show you what hidden, unmet needs he or she might have and how you might be able to meet of those needs.

3. "Practice hospitality." Make the person feel special with flowers or food he or she enjoys. Difficult as it may be, spend time just listening to him or her.

4. "Bless those who persecute you; bless and do not curse. . . . Do not repay anyone evil for evil. Be careful to do what is right in the eyes everybody." Remember your children aren't unaware of or insensitive to what is going on. What are you teaching them by your response?

5. "Do not be proud." Remember, you too may sometimes be difficult to live with.

6. "*If it is possible*, as far as it depends on you, live at peace." If all you try fails, try physically separating yourself from the person most of the time, but continue in hopeful, *faith*-full prayer.

> *When I am injured, help me to pardon, dear Lord.*
> *When I am tempted to despair, teach me to hope.*

Is there someone you find difficult to live with? Pray for that person, visualizing that person changed.

33

The View as We Look Back

"I can do everything through him who gives me strength" (Philippians 4:13).

They grow up so fast," sighed the young mother as she watched her daughter disappear into the classroom for the first day of kindergarten. Like many parents, she was having some internal struggles as her child entered a new phase of life.

On the one hand, the years of single parenting had not been easy. Balancing a job along with the full burden of parenting—not to mention trying to find time for a few private moments—had been grueling. There had been some days when she had wondered how she would ever make it.

But thanks to supportive family members, friends, and the church, she *had* made it. And yet now, looking back, she realized how much she had enjoyed those years with her child.

Our experiences can look much different when we look back on them from a later standpoint. And as we watch our children grow and change, we can be thankful for God's continuing care—at home, while traveling, and at school.

Dear God, thank you for the special times with my children. Give me the strength and hope I need when the going gets rough.

If you are a single parent, what resources are available to support you in your family, church, and community?

Let Need Fan Faith into a Blaze

"The woman came and knelt before him. 'Lord, help me!' she said" (Matthew 15:25).

Sometimes a person may have run into stormy waters before faith in God is kindled or rekindled in his or her heart. Until that time the tiny flame of faith may have burned only dimly, barely kept alive by routine or sporadic church attendance. Then tragedy strikes. All attention is directed to the One who can help.

The Canaanite woman who came to Jesus while he was on retreat in Lebanon reacted like that. Her daughter was severely possessed by a demon. It took courage for her to approach Jesus, however, because she was a despised Gentile. She wasn't sure who this Jew was, but the reports had been good, and she was desperate to try anything. Would this Gentile woman ever have bothered to come to Jesus if her child had not been harassed? Probably not. It was the illness of her child that brought this woman and Jesus together.

Desperate need can bring Jesus and us together too.

> My God, when cold, joyless winds blow through my life and soul, send your southwester of love and grace to melt my unbelief. Then warmed by your love, I shall be able to live with hope again.

Has some need caused you to seek Jesus? Seek on. Help will always come.

When God Seems to Ignore Us

"He answered, 'I was sent only to the lost sheep of Israel'" (Matthew 15:24).

Help didn't come quickly or easily for his mother with a stricken child. To begin with, Jesus ignored her and responded with silence. When she persisted, he reminded her that she was a Gentile, although he did it gently, using the word for dog that meant a little pet dog. She grabbed at the metaphor. "Even the little pet dogs get to eat the crumbs that fall from the family table," she said.

Delighted by her insistence and by her confidence, Jesus granted her request and then praised her for her faith. In the various steps Jesus took in dealing with this woman we see him wooing her, leading her gently on to ever greater and greater declarations of faith and trust.

Are you up against God's silence now? Has God seemed to refuse your request? Can you, like the woman, confess that you are not worthy of his grace but still ask for a few crumbs? Can you let God be who he is, sovereign God? And above all, can you go on trusting God? Silences are not always refusals. Silences may be invitations to more complete trust.

> My God, control my spirit's weather. When cold, joy-less, weary winds blow through my life and soul, be then to me my south wind, my summer wind.

Thinking back over your life, can you recall times when refusals actually became blessings?

Who's Educating Your Child?

"So the woman stayed at home and nursed her son until she had weaned him" (1 Samuel 1:23).

A woman asked a famous educator, "When should I begin to educate my child?"

"How old is your child?" the educator inquired.

"Five," the woman replied.

"Run home and begin now," stated the man. "You already have wasted five years."

Bible scholars believe Samuel was three or four when Hannah weaned him and then entrusted him to Eli's care. Until that time Hannah gave careful attention to caring for Samuel, and later the fruit was visible in the man Samuel became.

Giant steps toward educating a child can be taken in the home. A home that provides good books, a level of conversation that includes discussion of ideas, and answers to a child's questions offers significant education.

Educating a child also includes showing the child by the way we live, eat, sleep, talk, play, and work that God is first in our lives. Education of our children is an active, ongoing process, one of the most important things we do in our entire lifetime.

Make me a teacher with you, O Christ. Nothing else is worthy of the precious lives you have entrusted to my care.

What are you saying to your children and grandchildren by the way you live? How much time do you spend with them?

Are You Too Sometimes Deaf?

"Let us also go, that we may die with him" (John 11:16).

Come quickly! Lazarus is very ill." The message had come to Jesus from Mary and Martha, his good friends. But Jesus didn't go. His disciples were relieved, because to have gone to Judea would have been very risky.

Two days later Jesus said, "Let's go now. Lazarus is dead, but I will go to awaken him." The disciples were dumbfounded. Go to Judea? Wake up a dead man?

Calmly Jesus reassured them, but so obsessed with fear were the disciples that all they could focus on was the danger that awaited Jesus in Judea.

Finally, with gloom hanging heavily on his every word, Thomas said, "Let us also go that we may die with him."

Fear prevented the disciples from hearing what Jesus was saying. When we are fearful, we need to relax and hear God's comforting word.

O Christ, save me from crippling, weakening fear.
Instead help me hear you speaking peace to me.

Can you recall times when fear so possessed you that it was hard to hear what Jesus was saying? How did things work out? Is there something you fear now? Can you hear Jesus speaking words of assurance and peace to you?

Scared of What's Ahead?

"From that time on Jesus began to explain to his disciples that he must go . . . be killed and on the third day be raised to life" (Matthew 16:21).

Irvin Janis, a Yale University psychologist, conducted a series of experiments to find out how people reacted to the stress of major surgery. He divided people into three groups according to their levels of fear:

1. Lots of fear. Couldn't sleep. Worried a lot.

2. Moderate fear. Asked questions but accepted reassurance from the medical staff. Remained outwardly calm. Were able to read or engage in other diversions before surgery.

3. No fear evident. Constantly cheerful and optimistic. Slept soundly.

After surgery, however, Group 3 experienced almost as much difficulty handling stress as Group 1. Those in Group 3 hadn't expected the pain and discomfort, so they became angry, discouraged, and uncooperative. They worried and complained.

Jesus tried to prepare his disciples for the grief and bereavement they would experience when he would die by informing them ahead of time.

Do you foresee a major change ahead of you? Prepare for it by gathering as much information as possible, and prepare for it spiritually by setting aside extra time to pray. An informed, active mind and a trusting heart anchored in God will enable you to face wisely any major transition in life.

> Give me courage to face situations realistically. Make me willing to learn what lies ahead, and then, O my God, give me the pluck I shall need.

When have you realized that getting information ahead of time helped you adjust to change?

How to Be Utterly Miserable

"I am a woman who is deeply troubled" (1 Samuel 1:15).

She had a lot going for her: a husband who adored her and who did everything he could to make her happy; the freedom that comes with not having a houseful of children to care for, but the opportunity to love and enjoy children who lived close to her. Still she was not happy. In fact, she had become deeply depressed and had lost her appetite. True, her husband had a second wife who needled her constantly, but what made Hannah even more unhappy was the fact that she couldn't get pregnant.

God heard Hannah's continuing pleas and gave her a son. Sometimes, however, it doesn't work out as happily for us. Some women never conceive. Some conceive so often that they have no time or energy to do other things they would like to do. There may be other things we want very much but don't have.

When we are denied something that we want very much, we can make ourselves miserable by not relinquishing our wants and accepting what God and life offers us. Only as we relinquish, accept, and determine to make the most of what we have can we see a way out of our suffering and find peace.

Because, O God, I have little power to control all the things that happen to me, work in my heart to make me willing to seek you in all circumstances.

If there is something you have not been able relinquish and turn over to God, ask him to enable you to do so.

When Anger Flares

"In your anger do not sin" (Ephesians 4:26).

The week had been long and difficult, overcrowded with activities, guests, and preparations for festive days ahead. I was tired. Our grown children, home for a visit, had been busy running here and there, meeting old friends, shopping, and squeezing in time to bone up for exams that they would face when they returned to school. I understood this, but still I was tired. One innocent request from one of my children tipped the scales of patience for me and I blew my top.

My anger was greeted with anger. The encounter left both of us smoldering with resentment, still angry but also remorseful and guilty for saying things that should never have been said. Maybe some of what was said needed to be said, but not in anger.

Jesus' anger—and he was angry on occasion—was never self-centered. He never erupted because he felt someone had injured him. It is wrong to let anger get out of control, to verbally whip those who will not meet our demands, and in a rage to express our displeasure that things are not going our way. If we have sinned in our anger, the only appropriate Christian thing to do next is to confess our sin and ask for forgiveness.

> O loving God, let me not harbor anything in my heart
> that would grieve you.

Is there anyone of whom you need to ask forgiveness?

Prepare for the Drought

"Put on the full armor of God, so that when the day of evil comes, you may be able to stand your ground" (Ephesians 6:13).

The tiny creosote bush survives in the desert, when month after month no rain falls, by sucking up all the moisture it can during the brief spring months of rain showers. Then it coats its leaves with a thick, waxy coating so none of the moisture can escape.

Kathryn Koob, during her long, anxious months of imprisonment in Iran, found herself drawing repeatedly from her storehouse of Scripture and song memorized in her childhood and youth. As she tapped these resources, she grew in courage and faith.

If you have not made it a practice to memorize Scripture before, you can begin to do so while you are working around the house, driving the car, waiting to pick up the children, or in the post office or doctor's office. Choose a verse, write it on a card, meditate on it, memorize it. Do the same with a song. Build up your treasury. Help your children do the same. Then no matter what happens, you shall be like the creosote bush whose leaf does not wither even during long periods of drought.

> God, I thank you for your strengthening Word, for song and for memory. Help our family use these gifts that our lives may reflect your beauty.

Are you and your children memorizing Scripture and songs? If not, why don't you begin today?

Have the Kids Been Fighting Again?

"The Lord gives wisdom" (Proverbs 2:6).

Your blood pressure has been climbing during discussions at home. Your adolescents have waxed eloquent as they have denounced war and capitalism. They're so sure of their of their stance, and your husband has blown his top a couple of times because he's such a staunch and loyal American. You're about ready to outlaw all passionate speeches in favor of peace and harmony. Do you think that would do?

Would you rather have apathetic, listless children—youngsters tuned to their thoughts only, not loving others or their country enough to be critical? And does stifling conflict produce peace? When the pressure gets too great, won't the youngsters erupt in some less desirable way? A parent can say, "Shut up!" or "Think like I do," and the child may shut up and a type of peace may be achieved, but at what price?

Would it be wiser to encourage openness of expression? Disagreements can turn into positive experiences, because when we argue we stimulate one another. Those who disagree with us make us think. If we can learn that harmony is not the only thing to be prized, we can begin to welcome and listen dispassionately to fiery outbursts. Then growth can come to all of us.

> *All-wise God, help me understand that error opinion can be tolerated as long as freedom of reason is allowed to combat it.*

Can you agree to disagree in your family? Why or why not?

An Unmarried Mother

"Delight yourself in the Lord and he will give you the desires of your heart" (Psalm 37:4).

Simply having children does not necessarily make a woman a mother, nor does not having children prevent one from becoming a mother.

Marion Gould discovered that. Marion never married, never bore children, never realized her dream of a career in education or medicine. But she did become mother to five children and assume the role of a mother to many more.

Marion began her adult life working in an office to ease her parents' financial burden. Later she cared for her terminally ill father, and after he died she worked to pay the staggering medical bills while caring for her ailing mother.

Marion loved children and began a "Children's Church" on Sunday mornings. She sponsored a homeless, East Indian four-year-old girl, Seroj, writing her weekly and sending money for her support and education.

After Seroj grew up, Marion opened her arms once more, this time to support and nurture a homeless Korean child. In addition, she decided she could take care of three more Indian orphans!

"My life could have been a barren and defeated one, but I have found glorious joy and fulfillment in responding to Christ's call," Marion said.

Thank you, God, for all who care for little ones who need your love.

Has your home emptied of your own children? If you were to take other children into your home, where would you find them?

Is Working in the Kitchen Wasting Time?

"They said to him, 'John's disciples often fast and pray . . . but yours go on eating and drinking'" (Luke 5:33).

The Gospels abound in accounts of eating and feasting: the wedding at Cana, the meal at Zacchaeus's house, the hillside picnics for the crowds, Martha's spread, the barbecue brunch on the beach for the weary fishermen, and, most memorable, the Last Supper. Why all this eating and drinking?

Webster defines a feast as "a religious festival of rejoicing." Food is love. Working together to produce or earn food, preparing a meal together, eating together, and cleaning up after the meal can bond us together in love in a far firmer way than merely saying, "I love you," needful as that is too.

I think of my mother and how she had a hard time accepting my dishwasher. "When we wash dishes together, we talk," she used to say. "Now after the meal one person loads the dishwasher and the rest of us scatter." Mother was right. machines that perform chores for us are delightful, but they also can impoverish us. Better to let mealtimes be times of communal sharing.

> O God, help me see mealtime preparations as activities
> that bond our family together in love.

Is mealtime a bonding time for your family? In what ways? What can you do to steer conversation and maintain a happy tone during mealtime?

A Pilgrim People?

"But our citizenship is in heaven" (Philippians 3:20).

My husband, Luverne, and I stood outside a cave which tradition identifies as the place where Paul was imprisoned in Philippi.

"Philip of Macedon founded the city and gave it his name," Luverne said. "In Paul's day it was an outpost of the far-flung Roman empire. Retired Roman soldiers were stationed here to keep order. They brought a Roman flavor to this Greek city as they clattered up and down these cobblestones, red capes streaming out behind them, helmets and spears glittering in the sun. The Roman language was spoken, and Roman holidays and customs brought glitter and sparkle to the city. The Philippians were proud of their city. When they hauled Paul and Silas before the magistrate, they referred to them as Jews, while they spoke of themselves as 'us Romans' "(Acts 16:20-21).

Paul urged the Philippian Christians to remember that their citizenship was in heaven. Their perspective on life and their values and morals were different from those in whose midst they lived and worked.

Holy Spirit, alert me when you see the world squeezing me into its mold.

In what ways does your life reflect to your children that you and they are a "pilgrim people"?

Custody

"Rid yourselves of all malice and all deceit, hypocrisy, envy, and slander of every kind" (1 Peter 2:1).

A divorce and custody bring added challenges to the already difficult task of being a parent. In his book *I Wish Someone Understood My Divorce*, Harold Ivan Smith offers some guidance for maintaining the confidence of your children:

"*1. Don't try to be both parents to your children.* One good parent is better than two bad parents. *2. Be the parent that you are.* Don't try to be a buddy or a pal. *3. Accept your limitations.* You cannot get it all done. Do what you can. *4. Learn to nurture yourself.* You need time to breathe. Children who have already lost one parent cannot afford to lose a second one. *5. Let the child be a child.* A child is not a pseudo-adult or quasi-mate."

Dear God, strengthen me with your patience, love, and wisdom.

If you are a divorced parent, how might your actions toward your former spouse reflect the forgiving love of Christ?

A Lady Who Didn't Go To Pity Parties

"My grace is sufficient for you" (1 Corinthians 12:9).

The wedding banquet was almost over when a small boy cried out, "Look, daddy, the lady across the table from us doesn't have any hands!"

The lady, Dr. Anne Carlsen, for thirty years administrator of the Anne Carlsen Hospital/School for handicapped children in Jamestown, North Dakota, smiled at the boy. "I don't need them either, do I?" she asked. "See," and she picked up her coffee cup with the two stubs that serve as hands for her. To get around, Dr. Carlsen uses two artificial legs and crutches. She regards her handicaps courageously and realistically. "It's not easy to be handicapped," Dr. Carlsen admits, "but the attitude a person has counts for more than the adverse effects of the handicap."

All of us have some handicaps, something about ourselves or our bodies we wish were different. Whatever our physical defect, handicap, or illness, it need not cripple us. No life is so hard that we can't make it easier by the way we take it. As we are teachable, God can show us many ways we can live with our handicaps and overcome.

> O Christ, as I lean on your cross, let me not refuse my own. In bearing it, teach me to bear it with the strength, courage, and wisdom you give.

How are you dealing with your personal handicaps?

Seen from a Distance

"Now I know in part; then I shall know fully" (1 Corinthians 13:12).

It had been a difficult year. I wondered why so many disappointments, frustrations, and heartaches had intruded on our life. What good could possibly come of it all?

I welcomed an invitation to get away and visit friends in western Canada. "Let's go to Lake Louise in the Rockies," they suggested. I was delighted. Years ago my husband and I had whiled away many a carefree hour there.

It was early June, so the castlelike chateau at Lake Louise was not yet open. People were scurrying around, sweeping, dusting, and polishing, but we were allowed inside. We took an elevator to the top floor and stood at a window looking down at the lake from a distance. How different it looked from that vantage point! Seen through the arched window, nestled between snow and tree-covered mountains, it glistened in the sunlight, and the whole scene looked like a painting of rare beauty and wonder, complete in every detail and form.

Some other words Mother had said to me once came floating back: "Now that I am old, I can see all the events of my life falling gently into place. The puzzle that once was only a jumble of pieces is becoming a whole and complete picture."

Breathing a prayer of thanksgiving, I turned away from the window. I was ready to go home. I could be patient and wait to view my picture from a different perspective later on. I could wait for the pieces of my puzzle to fit together.

Loving God, when a valley lies before me, help me go through it believing that some day I shall be able to see the blessing it brought me.

As you think back over your life, in what ways has your perspective changed?

When Trouble Brews

"When his brothers saw that their father loved him more than any of them, they hated him and could not speak a kind word to him" (Genesis 37:4).

Conflict was brewing in the family, but Jacob didn't catch the warning signals. The older boys were jealous of their brother Joseph, who clearly was their father's favorite. They called their brother names: dreamer, "your son" in stead of "our brother." And when they sat around the campfire at night in their sheepfold, the older brothers gossiped and grumbled and aired their grievances.

Ordinarily parents tune in quickly when conflict among the children brews, but, in this case, Jacob missed it or ignored it until it was too late. The brothers took action into their own hands and got rid of the one who was irritating them.

Ignoring signals of internal conflicts in relationships in a family is dangerous. What would have happened if Jacob had called his sons together and asked what was eating away at them? Suppose the older boys had felt free to ask their father why he liked Joseph better than them? Suppose Jacob had been humble and wise enough to have seen his fault and done something about it? In the end God turned evil into good, but believing God can do this does not excuse us from dealing with internal conflict when it first rears its head.

Alert me when trouble is brewing, wise God, and then give me courage and understanding to deal with it.

How do you deal with internal conflict of relationships in your family?

What's Wrong with Dreaming?

"Joseph had a dream" (Genesis 37:5).

Though Joseph's dream was fantastic and even arrogant, it did eventually come true. But first Joseph had to experience alienation from his brothers, the horror of the pit, the terror of being carried away by strangers, the bewildering adjustment to a new people, land, language, and culture, and then, for no fault of his, a jail sentence. Only after all this did Joseph's dream come true.

As a child I dreamed of wings I could put on and fly anywhere. Perhaps my dream was partially realized in my adult years by all the flying around the world I've done. My writing, too, was a postponed dream.

Our children dream. Some discover as they emerge into adulthood that the need to earn a living will curb, shape, frustrate, and change many of their dreams. As mothers we have a double task: to safeguard a period of carefree childhood when our children can dream, while at the same time teaching them to distinguish between fantasy and reality. Otherwise they may be overwhelmed by their search to find work that both satisfies and provides adequate support for them. Parents help their children when they pray for them, love them, and seek wisdom to respond appropriately to them.

Dear God, give me wisdom as I encourage our children to dream.

What dreams have you seen realized? What can you do to help unrealized ones come true?

Our Children's Friends

"He has gone to be the guest of a 'sinner' " (Luke 19:7).

What had prepared Jesus to be as accepting as he was of people of different backgrounds, cultures, values, and habits? Where had he learned this openness?

Usually children learn most from their parents and their peers. The Gospels do not tell us specifically, so we can only wonder how much Jesus' mother had influenced him. We think of the circumstances that must have had some part in shaping her. Had enduring an unusual pregnancy and hearing the whisperings that went on made her more tolerant toward the misunderstood? Had the years in Egypt living among people of a different culture, religion, and language also enabled her to see the person behind his or her outer facade?

How is it for you? When your children bring home friends whose values, habits, dress, and manners are vastly different from yours, how do you react?

"When my son came home with a girlfriend of another race, I had to steel myself not to let my feelings show," a mother said. "But during the weekend, as I learned to know her, I found myself appreciating and liking her."

Increase, O gentle Savior, my patience, tolerance, and understanding.

Have you ever discovered you had a mistaken idea about someone?

When Interruptions Upset Plans

"Jesus . . . withdrew by boat privately to a solidarity place. Hearing of this, the crowds followed him on foot from the towns" (Matthew 14:13).

Jesus had his disciples row him across the lake, but when he got there he discovered that people had come running by foot and were there waiting for him. Jesus turned the interruption into an opportunity to preach to an overflowing crowd and then afterward treated them to dinner. As we read the Gospels we note the many interruptions that intruded into Jesus' life. And in every case we see how instead of resenting the interruptions he used them.

Sometimes it seems as though we can't get away from it all either. Our schedules may be so hectic that it seems as if all of life is interruptions.

Henri Nouwen tells of an older professor at Notre Dame University who said to him with a certain melancholy in his voice, "You know . . . my whole life I have been complaining that my work was constantly interrupted, until I discovered that my interruptions were my work."

> Because, O God, I have little power to control all the things that happen to me, work in my heart to make me willing to seek you in all circumstances.

Can you recall an incident when you were able to regard an interruption as an opportunity? For one week try turning interruptions into opportunities and record in your journal what happened.

What Does God Think of Women?

"The angel went to her and said, 'Greetings, you who are highly favored! The Lord is with you'" (Luke 1:28).

There are many disagreements in the church today about the role of women. Some think we should stick to traditional roles, others want to see more women in leadership positions. Both sides often quote the Bible to support their positions.

But no matter what we decide about women's roles, we need to be clear about our "role" in God's eyes. We need to be reminded that God loves and accepts us just as we are, regardless of our station in life, calling, or career.

One of the great ironies in the Bible is the role that Mary played in the story of salvation. At the time when Jesus was born, women had a very low status in Judaism. They had few rights and were not even allowed to sit in the same part of the synagogue as the men. In court, the word of a woman carried very little weight.

And yet God chose Mary—a lowly woman of Galilee—to be the mother of the Savior of the world. God gave women the greatest honor possible by choosing one to become the vehicle through whom God, incarnate in Christ, would enter the world.

Thank you, God, for choosing to be born of a woman, and for honoring all mothers through your choice of Mary.

What has being a mother meant to you?

Permissible Responses to Anger

"When Moses approached the camp and saw the calf and the dancing, his anger burned" (Exodus 32:19).

The Israelites had been acting like spoiled children, ungrateful for what God had done for them in freeing then from Pharaoh. Instead, they complained and grumbled, and nothing pleased them.

Moses had been patient, but when he saw the golden calf they had made in his absence, it was too much. The people were rejecting God, preferring to be slaves rather than free people, loving darkness more than light.

Moses vented his anger, and it was appropriate for him to do so because the people had sinned against God. Anger that occurs for the right reasons can be used for good, and sometimes it can help to bring about change for the better.

However, it takes prayer and the enlightenment of the Holy Spirit to discern the reasons behind our anger: Are we angry because God is being opposed, or is it because we feel attacked, misused, and wronged, or because we feel out of control? If we ask, God will give us wisdom and help us express our anger in appropriate ways.

> O God of justice and love, when I get angry, teach me
> to respond appropriately.

What kinds situations have you found difficult to handle? Talk to the Lord about these and ask for guidance.

One Secret of Being Happy

"Dorcas . . . was always doing good and helping the poor" (Acts 9:36).

Dorcas probably was a widow. We read that at her death all the widows stood around Paul "crying and showing him the robes and other clothing that Dorcas had made while she was still with them." As a widow, Dorcas could have moped and felt sorry for herself. She could have lived in the past. Instead, she chose to reach out and in doing so became loved and honored.

Eleanor Roosevelt once counseled, "Think as little as possible about yourself, and as much as possible about other people. You will get more joy out of giving joy to others, and you should put a good deal of thought into the happiness that you are able to give."

The Lord Jesus modeled for this pattern of forgetting ourselves in caring about others. Even in the tortured hours of his betrayal and crucifixion we find him praying for others, healing a soldier, comforting a dying man, and providing for the loving care of his mother.

> O Christ, free me from being self-centered. May I know in fuller measure the joy that comes when I reach out to bring happiness to others.

Does caring for others mean that mothers give no thought to their own needs? How do you keep the two in balance?

Gracious Patterns

"Follow my example, as I follow the example of Christ" (1 Corinthians 11:1).

A group of psychologists conducted an experiment in which children could watch adults bowl. The possibilities of points ranged from five to thirty. When one group of adults scored twenty or more, they helped themselves to some chocolates in a dish. "We deserve it," they said. When they scored lower, they said, "No candy reward for us." A second group of adults watched by another group of children rewarded themselves when they scored ten or higher. Then the children were allowed to play, and in each case, they followed the pattern of the adults they had observed. A third group of children, who had observed no adults at play, helped themselves indiscriminately to the candy.

As a Christian mother, I want my children to become like Christ. Will that be possible if they imitate me? Must I not then seek to be like Christ? And how can do I do that? We become like others by observation and imitation. I can observe Christ by studying his Word. And as I see other Christians living as Christ has taught us to live, I can seek to pattern my life after theirs.

Give us, O God, grace in speech and love in deed and free us from wrongful thoughts and actions.

Who do you esteem as a Christian? Who helps you in your Christian walk?

Why Write Letters?

"Like cold water to a weary soul is good news from a distant land" (Proverbs 25:25).

I cleaned the bedrooms one last time, then shut the doors. All the children were off to college. Already I was missing them.

I keep in touch, of course. They call. I write letters. For wonderful as it is to hear voices, telephone conversations, at best, linger only uncertainly and temporarily in the memory. Letters can be read and reread. But letter writing is an art. I like to turn to that prolific and marvelous correspondent, Paul, for guidelines.

He expressed appreciation. He thanked his readers for all they had done for him and meant to him. He shared personal news. At the same time he shared his testimony as to how he had seen God work in situations. He also shared his struggles. He let them know his concern for them by referring to the troubles and problems they were experiencing. And he dared suggest some ways out! He told them he loved them and was lonesome for them. But he also corrected them when they needed it. His letters were positive, joyful, and affirming. He appealed to them to rise to the highest God had for them.

Wise God, save me from writing or speaking words that wound. Instead teach me to comfort, encourage or support.

Is there someone you should write or call today?

Developing Perseverance

"Consider it pure joy . . . whenever you face trials of many kinds, because you know that the testing of your faith develops perseverance" (James 1:2).

Six months had passed since Joan and Ray, divorced parents, had married and joined their families. Joan was in tears. "I don't think it will work," she sobbed.

"I've had plenty of moments when I've thought the same," her friend Barbara said. "There're plenty of us struggling."

"But I've never felt like such a complete failure," Joan wailed. "I never used to be as irritable as I am now."

"Your task is harder," Barb said. "And being irritated with each other isn't such a threat to family solidarity when the children are your own flesh and blood. You belong to each other whether you like you like it or not at the moment, so you feel safe in letting off a little steam. Not so with the children of your new husband, or your husband. Your relationship with them is tenuous, and you fear the effect your irritableness might have on them. Understand this. Let them know your fears and be patient. Allow time for growth. It will come as surely as spring follows winter if you trust God to lead. You're not alone in this. Remember that."

Loving, patient God, help me use disappointments as material for patience.

If life is tough for you these days, don't hesitate to ask for help.

That Fantastic Thing Called Love

"While he was still a long way off, his father saw and was filled with compassion for him; he ran to his son, threw his arms around him and kissed him" (Luke 15:20).

His kid brother had come home broke after squandering all their father had given him. Talk about nerve! And their father was throwing a party for him! The elder son exploded, "Look! All these years I've been slaving for you, and I've never disobeyed your orders." Here was the aggrieved complaining of someone who feels he has been taken advantage of but hasn't dared rebel.

"You never gave me a party." Maybe not. But did all else the father had given count for nothing?

And then the elder son accused the father of being stupid by throwing a party. How did the son think the father should have greeted the younger son? With a tongue lashing? With an order to clear out of the house? The father had plenty reason to be angry with both sons. Instead he let love spill out.

Occasions to freely forgive undeserving children, to speak kindly to rude children, and to welcome home penniless young adult children will come again and again. Only God can enable us to receive them as he receives us. But God can and will, if we but open ourselves to him.

Gracious God, help us realize that love is given to us to give away.

If you had been the parent, would you have kissed or scolded? Explain.

Who Is Molding You?

"Do not conform any longer to the pattern of this world, but be transformed by the renewing of your mind" (Romans 12:2).

My parents never really talk to me. They don't know how I feel about things. I try to talk to my dad but he's usually listening to news or watching a game, and he says, 'Uh, huh,' or 'I'm tired. Tell me tomorrow.' Mom says the same."

We had been talking about family life, and only two or three of the young people in my ninth-grade Bible class said they felt their parents had time for them.

In addressing the subject of the breakdown of family life development John H. Knowles, president of the Rockefeller Foundation, said, "One thing that is hurting family life is everybody's being glued to that God-forsaken TV."

What place does the TV have in your family? How much of your time does it consume? To what extent are your values and the values of your family being shaped by it? Could you live without it?

Help us, God, to consider these questions seriously, respond truthfully, and then act obediently.

Try to go one whole month without watching TV. At the end, discuss in what ways your family life changed.

Compulsive Overwork?

" 'Martha, Martha,' the Lord answered, 'You are worried and upset about many things'" (Luke 10:41).

Mary's sister, Martha, reacted differently. All this death talk that Jesus was doing really upset her. She disappeared into the kitchen. Best to drown worries in work, she may have thought.

Perhaps Martha overstretched herself and planned too elaborate a menu, and there were too many things to watch at one time. Her patience snapped. She stormed in and attacked the two people whom she loved the most. "Neither of you care about me!" she implied. Poor, frightened, frustrated, worried, insecure Martha!

Jesus' words were both perceptive and tender. "Martha, Martha, you are worried and upset about too many things." It was as if Jesus was saying, "It's not the meal that's bothering you most, Martha. What makes you work so feverishly? What are you worried about?" Then by commending Mary's actions, Jesus indicated that taking the time to be taught by him is more important than many other things.

Does anxiety drive you to compulsive overwork sometimes? Or are you willing to face your anxieties and be taught by God?

Enable me to cast all my cares on you, O God.

Sometime work is helpful in alleviating tension. When does it cease to be helpful?

Win Respect, Love May Follow

"By wisdom a house is built, and through understanding it is established" (Proverbs 24:3).

I don't think Jeff will ever love me," Phil said, his voice flat and lifeless. "I've tried everything I could think of—taken him fishing, bought him a new bike, increased his allowance. And what thanks do I get for it? Sassy talk," he sighed.

Phil mistakenly had hoped to win his stepson's affection by gushing over him, giving lavishly to him, and trying to please him. What Phil hadn't understood was that a stepparent's first task is not to win the love of his new children, but to win their respect.

It may be that the children will never choose to refer to their stepfather as "father." They may want, instead, for him to be a friend. But whatever form the relationship finally takes, the stepparent's first goal must be to win respect.

Respect is won when the new parent helps enforce rules and maintain order. The child also needs to see consistent loving behavior on the part of the new parent. The child must come to believe that he or she can trust the new parent. When respect is won, love often begins to grow.

> O Holy Spirit, give us wisdom to act and speak in such a way that our children will respect us.

Have your parents won your respect? How did this happen?

Practicing the Presence of God

"I was hungry and you gave me something to eat" (Matthew 25:35).

Catherine of Siena, a Christian of the 1300s, thought that being with Jesus meant giving herself to prayer, meditation, and fasting. So when she was 16, she shut the door of her room and concentrated on a devotional life. At the end of three years she emerged. Carefully she began to help with household chores and to visit the sick and poor. The Lord had told her, she said, that she would grow closer to him as she ministered to others and sought the fellowship of other Christians.

This did mean that she gave up her times of devotion. She knew that they were a source of strength. But she recognized that as she served others she would bring honor to God. As she gave of herself and received from other Christians, she would be experiencing the presence of God with her.

If we as mothers practice the presence of God with us as we clean, launder, cook, and care for our families, our homes can take on an aura of peace and happiness which others will feel when they come to our home. God will be glorified.

Lord Jesus, help me to know your presence with me
daily to a greater degree than I now know.

Today consciously practice the presence of God with you. At the end of the day think as to what difference this has made.

Do You Feel Confined at Home?

"Some women were watching from a distance. Among them were Mary Magdelene, Mary the mother of James the younger and of Joses, and Salome. In Galilee these women had followed him and cared for his needs" (Mark 15:40-41a).

We know little about this little cluster of women huddled together in common sorrow near the cross. The few words written about them tell us, however, that they had been present enough with Jesus to have become known by name to the men with Jesus.

Mary and Salome were mothers. We can presume they were middle-aged or older. They must have been a bit radical for their day, for instead of staying home they had begun to follow Jesus wherever he went. They cared for him, perhaps by cooking his meals, doing his laundry, or arranging for places where he could stay.

As we read church history, we find recorded the names of many women who were honored as leaders in the church. These women recognized the various gifts God had given them and used them. Their ministries stretched beyond their homes. Do ours?

O God, may we be honest in owning the gifts you have given us and faithful in using them.

What gifts has God given you? How are you using them in service to God and others?

Is the Best Always Saved to the Last?

"When you pass through the waters, I will be with you; and when you pass through the rivers, they will not sweep over you" (Isaiah 43:2).

James Limburg, a seminary professor, tells of a conversation he had with a visitation pastor who had been calling on the aged. After reflecting for a while on the aging process, the pastor said, "I've learned that the Lord saves . . ." and he paused. Limburg expected him to say ". . . the best to the last." Instead the pastor said, ". . . the hardest part until the last."

As we watch our parents age, we may feel like repeating those words if we stand helplessly by, watching them weaken and sustain loss of memory, vision, hearing, or bodily control. How good to know we are not alone! The suffering Savior stands by our side and our parents' side. He is with us. The waters will not overwhelm us or them.

> *O merciful Father, we do not believe that you willingly afflict your children. Look with mercy on the sorrows and troubles of our loved ones for whom we now pray. Strengthen them in patience. Comfort them with the memory of your goodness to them in times past. Let your presence be felt by them, and give them peace through Jesus Christ our Lord.*

Are aging people part of your family circle? Are your children learning to love, respect, and care for the aging?

Beautiful Inside and Out

"Repent and believe in the good news!" (Mark 1:15).

An executive in the cosmetics industry said, "Make a woman beautiful on the outside and she will become beautiful inside." Is this true? Jesus spoke of people who had lovely exteriors while inside they were like rotting corpses (Matthew 23:27). Rotting insides need a miracle if the person is to become a truly beautiful person. So when Jesus began his ministry, he picked up John the Baptist's message and urged people to repent.

"Turn around," he pleaded. "Face the other direction. Head toward God. Experience a change of mind as to what is right and important in life."

But because finger wagging alone is ineffective, as all naggers know, Jesus added, "And believe in the gospel."

The good news that God has forgiven us makes us into new persons who radiate the love of God.

> O God of love, when I willfully wander away from you, even though I know you love me, turn me around.

Can you name someone in whom the beauty of God can be clearly seen?

Loving with Common Sense

"I press on toward the goal" (Philippians 3:14).

Do you ever feel that being a worthy wife, mother, mother-in-law, or grandmother is far more difficult and demanding than you imagined it to be? Do you lament the fighting and squabbling that sometimes goes on between your children? Do you sometimes feel like shipping them off to someone else?

Maybe some of these feelings come because of unrealistic expectations we have coveted for our family. Maybe it is time to listen to some wise words from another parent, Anne Morrow Lindbergh:

"When you love others, you do not love them all the time, in exactly the same way, from moment to moment," she wrote. "It is an impossibility. It is even a lie to pretend to. And yet that is exactly what most of us demand. We have so little faith in the ebb and flow of life, love, of relationships. We leap at flow of the tide and withdraw in terror when it ebbs. . . . Security in a relationship lies in the present relationship and accepting it as it is now."

> *Patient God of understanding and love, teach me to love with common sense.*

All of us from time to time expect behavior from our children that is unreasonable given the circumstances. When this has happened in your case, how have you handled it? In what ways did your parents make unreasonable demands? How did you react?

Don't Let Success Destroy You

"Very early in the morning, while it was still dark, Jesus got up, left the house and went off to solitary place, where he prayed" (Mark 1:35).

What was troubling Jesus so that he got up so early to be by himself and pray? What did he pray about? We don't know. We only know what preceded this prayer time: Jesus had become an immediate smashing success. Crowds came. Jesus could chalk up visible results.

"Everyone is looking for you," his friends said. It was enough to turn anyone's head.

Jesus knows that unless we get alone where we can hear God speak to us, we're headed for trouble. Success is heady, whether we experience it in our careers or our husbands do in theirs. Few can handle it. Only as we meet God alone do we remember our appropriate attitude and response: "We are unworthy servants; we have only done our duty" (Luke 17:10).

> O purest Wisdom, when you grant success to our efforts, let us not forget to continue to dwell in your Word and live in obedience to it.

Why is success so filled with danger?

After the Funeral Is Over

"Near the cross of Jesus stood his mother . . . and Mary of Magdala" (John 19:25).

We find the two of them together at the cross: Mary, the mother of the one who is dying, and Mary from Magdala, the devoted follower whom the dying one had made whole.

We do not know their relationship to each other. It could have been one of tension, for the mother had difficulty accepting what her son was doing, and the other Mary was one of his most ardent supporters. Each could have looked at the other with suspicion, but instead they wept together as the one they loved died.

The death of a loved one sometimes brings together family members who have differed with each other. At funeral services, plunged in sorrow, they sit side by side.

What happens after the funeral service can determine future relationships. The fissures of separation can split open even wider. On the other hand, broken relationships can be healed as hearts made tender become receptive to open, honest communication, sometimes followed by confession and forgiveness. Happiest are those, however, who are reconciled before funerals take place.

O Holy Spirit, help me to let you search my heart.

Is there someone with whom you need to be reconciled? Can you take the first step today?

The Right to Be Wrong

"The younger son . . . squandered his wealth in wild living" (Luke 15:13).

Before giving the younger son the inheritance he requested, I'm sure the father begged his son to think carefully about the wisdom of what he wanted to do. I can feel the father's heavy heart as he watched his son walk off.

But what else could the father have done? If he had refused, would his rebellious son have stayed home and made life miserable for all, or perhaps walked off, angry but determined to make it on his own? The relationship in any case would have been broken.

Instead the father granted his son's request. Why? Because the father knew a time comes in everyone's life when he or she has a "right to be wrong." This "right" does not make a wrong decision right or absolve the consequences of wrong choices. Maturity and independence involve decision-making and always carry the potential of error, whether deliberate or not.

I can imagine the father standing at the gate day after day, peering down the road, wondering when his son would come back home for a visit. Did he know in what condition his son would return? We don't know, but he soon found out, and then he had to make another decision.

When my children make decisions I think are unwise, I need extra grace from you, O God of all forbearance and understanding. Help me to let them go, but you go with them and care for them.

What foolish decisions have you made in your life? What was the outcome?

Why Do We Give Gifts?

"Each year his [Samuel's] mother made him a little robe and took it to him when she went up with her husband to offer the annual sacrifice" (1 Samuel 2:18).

Hannah had entrusted her son to be raised and trained by Eli in the temple, and she lived so far away that she saw him only once a year. Between visits imagine her sitting and working on a little robe, stitching in her love and prayers, embroidering it to make it the finest she could. See her preparing for the journey, wrapping the robe and feeling joy at the thought of being able to give it to her son. And picture the reunion: the rush to embrace, the sustained hugging, Hannah holding Samuel away so she can gaze at him and see how he has grown. Now she reaches behind her and with both hands extends her gift. His eyes sparkle in expectation. She watches smiling as he carefully unwraps the robe, shakes it out, and then runs off to try it on. Samuel comes back, walking very straight, so proud of his new robe. And Hannah's chin quivers. Her eyes mist over as she says, "What a handsome lad you have become!"

Divorced parents and grandparents often live so far from children and grandchildren that they see them only occasionally. When distances separate, extra effort should be made to establish and maintain caring relationships. One of the best ways is by giving a gift. The gift need not be great. It is always the spirit and the manner in which a gift is given that gives it it's worth.

O God, giver of all good gifts and giver of yourself, thank you for all you have given me. Thank you also that I can give.

When did someone give a gift to you that was especially meaningful? Why?

What Lands Us in Hot Water?

"Preserve sound judgment and discernment, do not let them out of your sight" (Proverbs 3:21).

In a cartoon two young children are watching their mom boil spaghetti. One remarks, "It's pasghetti. You have to boil it to get it to relax."

Landing in hot water has the opposite effect on us. We tighten up and get tense. What causes us to get all hot and bothered? Having too much to do for one thing, many mothers declare. Perhaps we need to ask why our lives tend to become overloaded.

In the first place, we aren't content with a simple life. We want more and more, and things cost money. To earn money, we have to work and do more work.

We also are pressured to "develop every talent." Ridiculous! There is no way any one of us will be able to this.

We hunger for recognition and rewards, and usually these come only when we are "active" and "involved," and usually outside of the home.

Life presents us with boundless opportunities for pleasure and fun. None of these things we've mentioned is bad, but too much of any can cause overload. We need God's gifts of sound judgment and discernment.

Give me wisdom, O God, to understand what I need to lighten my load.

Do you feel you have too much to do? What could you eliminate?

Who Sets the Limitations?

"If you are able! . . . All things are possible for the one who believes" (Mark 9:23).

A father was up against an agonizing situation in which he felt utterly helpless to aid his son. But because he loved his child, he couldn't quit.

Love never gives up. Only when the flame of love has been extinguished do we give up. But the father had been disappointed so many times that he was cautious in his request. "If you can do anything, I'd appreciate it," he said to Jesus.

Jesus will not be reduced by humans to puny size. "If you are able!" he exclaimed. Then he threw the responsibility back where it belonged, and said, in effect, "I'm not the one who has the limitations. It's you, because you don't really believe I am who I am or that I can do what I can do."

What bracing words for us to face as difficult situations confront us! Who do we say Jesus is? What do we believe he can do for us?

Lord, I do believe. Help my unbelief.

What do you wish Jesus would do for you? Talk with him about this.

The Value of Rules

"You have laid down precepts that are to be fully obeyed" (Psalm 119:4).

I've never liked you!" Norma yelled at her sister.

"What makes you think I like you? I've tried and tried to be nice to you and you just ignore me," Fern snapped.

People in the same family do not necessarily like each other, but they still have to learn to live together in harmony. To help achieve harmony, parents, from the start, need to come to an agreement regarding rules. Rules should be clearly stated. Writing and posting them helps. After they are learned, they can be taken down.

In a blended family, children are more apt to follow the rules if the biological parent draws up rules regarding homework, sleep, eating, friends, etc. But the stepparent needs to help enforce them.

Children will try to pit one parent against another. If parents maintain control, they can't allow this.

Parents also need to strive for consistency in enforcing the rules. Children may try to wear down parents, but parents can't afford to let weariness or busyness cause them to relax the rules.

As rules are made and enforced, order and harmony begin to happen, and in this soil love can also grow.

Teach our family to love and respect your law, O God.

Are rules clearly defined and regularly enforced in your family?

Hard to Keep Quiet

"If I say, 'I will not mention him, or speak any more in his name,' his word is in my heart like a burning fire, shut up in my bones. I am weary of holding it in; indeed, I cannot" (Jeremiah 20:9).

Eliaiki Kalugila of Tanzania, East Africa, is a mother of seven. In addition to caring for her children and her husband, she is in charge of a preschool. In spite of these heavy responsibilities, on many Sundays Eliaiki gathers a group of women and goes to an outlying area where people still do not know much about the Lord Jesus. There the women sing and preach, teach and talk.

They return home when the sun begins to kiss good-bye to the trees—as they say there—weary but refreshed, contented and happy. Why? Because these women witness and proclaim out of a sense of vocation. The love of Christ compels them. They *want* to. They voluntarily choose to do so. And the radiant smiles on their faces bear witness to the joy they find.

> Give us, O Christ, hearts of love and tongues of fire
> to witness—without embarrassment or hesitancy, but
> with joy—to what you have done for us.

What opportunities do you find for witnessing and proclaiming what Christ Jesus has done for you and means to you?

Greedy Over Inheritances?

"Watch out! Be on your guard against all kinds of greed" (Luke 12:15).

When a man asked Jesus to settle a family dispute about an inheritance, Jesus refused. Instead he told a parable warning against greed. Note all the pronouns referring to the man in the story, revealing how self-centered and self-confident he is. Observe that his thought is only for this present life.

During the early years of adult life in particular, and sometimes again at the end of life, our concern is that we shall not have enough. But after we have been working for a while promotions come, and we may become greedy. Possessions and pleasure are like peanuts—the more you eat, the more you want. Advertisers feed that hunger. Enough never seems enough for us, either personally or as a favored nation.

Greed can enter when families distribute inheritances. But no matter what we may receive from an inheritance, what will it be worth if it results in broken relationships? Jesus encourages us, instead, to be rich toward God.

Help us, O God, to live with eternity's values in view.

Has acquisitiveness gotten a hold on you? If so, what can you do about it?

Who Does He Think He Is?

"When you give a luncheon or dinner, do not invite your friends . . ." (Luke 14:12).

The party was over; the guest were gone. The hostess was furious. For some reason, the guests hadn't waited for her husband to seat them. Instead, everyone had scrambled for the places of honor. That was embarrassing enough, but then Jesus called it to everyone's attention that they should wait for others to recognize their worth.

They had deserved the rebuke, the hostess thought, but still it was embarrassing to have Jesus confront them so directly. And then Jesus had gone after her! How audacious to suggest that she should invite the crippled the lame and the blind!

We often think of Jesus only as the one who comforts us in times of need, the one who accepts us unconditionally. He certainly does do those things, but he is also a Lord who can make us extremely uncomfortable. During his earthly ministry he rebuked both friends and foes alike when they stood against God's will.

Yes, Jesus is the loving Savior. But he is also a Lord who makes his commanding presence felt in our lives.

Lord Jesus, help me hear your correction and challenge
to my behavior as well as the good news of your love.

Read Luke 14:1-14, putting yourself in the place of the hostess of the party. How would you feel if this happened to you?

Are Hurt Feelings Sometimes Necessary?

"Whoever does God's will is my brother and sister and mother" (Mark 3:20-35).

Jesus' response when he was told that his family had come to see him seems insensitive and unloving. He appears to deny his relationship to them.

To understand his retort, we need to consider the preceding verses. His friends were fearing that Jesus had become irrational and deranged (v.21). Had this rumor reached Jesus' family? Had they come to bring him home? To protect him from danger? Or to keep him from making a fool of himself or of them? They could not understand why he was doing what he was doing.

Sometimes our loved ones do not understand when we hear Christ's call. The wealthy father of 23-year-old Perpetua, one of the early Christian martyrs, pleaded with her to recant and deny Christ. She refused. But, she said, to displease her father caused her more pain that the prospect of death. It was a price she had to pay to be true to Christ.

Hurting the feelings of his family when they wanted to divert him from his mission was a price Jesus, too, had to pay on his way to Jerusalem.

> O Christ, when pressures from others would veer us
> away from you, save us. May we grow in knowledge of
> your love so we shall want to stay close to you.

Has your family ever asked you to do something you felt was not acceptable for a Christian to do? How did you handle the situation? How did it work out?

Children Learn What They Live With

"Set an example for the believers in life, in love, in faith, and in purity" (1 Timothy 4:12).

> If a child lives with criticism,
>   He learns to condemn.
> If a child lives with hostility,
>   He learns to fight.
> If a child lives with ridicule,
>   He learns to be shy.
> If a child lives with shame,
>   He learns to feel guilty.
> If a child lives with tolerance,
>   He learns to be patient.
> If a child lives with encouragement,
>   He learns confidence.
> If a child lives with praise,
>   He learns to appreciate.
> If a child lives with fairness,
>   He learns justice.
> If a child lives with security,
>   He learns to have faith.
> If a child lives with approval,
>   He learns to like himself.
> If a child lives with acceptance and friendship,
>   He learns to find love in the world.
>   —Author unknown

Dear God, give us calm strength and patient wisdom, to teach our children to love whatever is just and true and good.

Who encouraged and gave you a sense of security as a child? Who criticized, ridiculed, or made you feel guilty? How have you found healing?

Love So Amazing

"But the father said to his servants, 'Quick! Bring the best robe and put it on him . . . Let's have a feast and celebrate' " (Luke 15:22, 23).

After the son had blown, not only his own savings but the money his parents had carefully put aside for his future, how could the father welcome back so lovingly his foolish, child limping home, dirty, in rags, penniless, and stinking from the pigpens? Wouldn't it have been sufficient if the father had said, "All right, we'll let you use your old room again. You don't deserve it, but it wouldn't look good in front of the neighbors if I turned you away. But get this straight! I want you to find a job immediately and work and save so you can pay back what you squandered"? What on earth motivated the father instead to embrace his son, take him to the store, buy him a new wardrobe—the finest he could find—and then throw a party in his honor? What motivates parents to forgive and forgive and forgive their children? Is it not love? Is there any other answer? As Barbara Lazear Archer, lawyer and writer, wrote, "Like being in love, being in love with a child colors things. You aren't to be trusted. Everything is a bit more than it seems. Everything seems a bit more than it is."

That is the way God loves us too, and that is why we are able to love our children. "True love's the gift God has given to humans alone," wrote Sir Walter Scott. "It is . . . the silver link, the silken tie, which heart to heart and mind to mind in body and in soul can bind."

O God of love, I cannot thank you enough for your amazing love. May it always flow through me also to others.

What instances can you recall when you have been loved by someone when you haven't deserved to be loved?

How Wide Is Your World?

"At that time Jesus came from Nazareth in Galilee and was baptized by John in the Jordan" (Mark 1:9).

After years of supporting his mother and brothers at the carpenter bench it was time for Jesus to leave home. He was ready to begin a new phase of his life. I wonder how Mary felt as she laundered his clothes, packed his bag, kissed him goodbye, and sent him on his way.

Mary had been introduced in her younger years to the wider world. She journeyed to Jerusalem to visit Elizabeth and then later, in advanced pregnancy, to Bethlehem. From there she went on to Egypt. in later life this view was stretched even further, for tradition tells us that when persecution began, John took her to the safety of Ephesus, a Greek city in present-day Turkey.

Did Mary think of how her own worldview had been widened as she watched her firstborn son set off? Did that produce joyous anticipation for the stretching experience that was to become his? That can happen to us when our children leave home, if we have experienced our world stretched wider.

Widen my world, O God.

How can reading and close contact with people of other ethnic backgrounds widen our worldview?

A Harvest of Righteousness

"No discipline seems pleasant at the time, but painful. Later on, however, it produces a harvest of righteousness and peace" (Hebrews 12:11).

Keeping the proper balance between discipline and forbearance is a challenge for parents. When discipline is too quick or too severe, children suffer. (And it is all too easy to cross the line from the harsh discipline into child abuse.) But when discipline is lax or absent, children become spoiled and do not learn necessary limits.

Martin Luther said, "One must punish in such a way that the rod is accompanied by the apple. It's a bad thing if children and pupils lose their spirit on account of their parents and teachers." He made that statement in the 16th century, when children had few rights and were often beaten in ways that today would quickly attract police intervention.

Sometimes it takes the wisdom of a Solomon to know how to discipline properly. But above all, children must not be treated in ways that make them doubt their parents' love or the love of God. With God, forgiveness is always the *final* word.

Dear God, help me learn to discipline in a loving, yet firm way.

Ask a trusted friend to observe you with your children and offer their impressions of how you are relating to each other.

Help for the Fainthearted

"He will come to us like the winter rains, like the spring rains that water the earth" (Hosea 6:3).

The assurance that he was acting in his Father's will acted like a steadying anchor and a guiding rudder for Jesus.

What gives *us* staying power? What enables us to keep hanging in when we want to give up? What keeps us believing when it seems futile to believe? What enables us to find joy in circumstances that we thought we couldn't even tolerate?

More than anything else isn't it the conviction that we are doing our Father's will?

The place is not too important. Nazareth was the right place for Jesus for 30 years. After that it was the road. Even our work is not the most important. Carpentry, if God calls us to it, is as sacred as preaching. So is sewing, teaching, fixing breakfasts, or working in an IRS office.

God's call is not as much a call to specific place or job as it is a call to live and walk with him. We may sometimes be unsure of where we are going, but it is enough to know we are on the way. The secret of where our going will lead us rests with the One who said, "Go." Because we know he loves us and we love him, we can follow unafraid.

> O most loving Father, you want us to fear nothing
> except losing you. Protect us from faithless fears.

Can you recall a time when you were tempted to give up? What enabled you to persevere?

Our Highest Calling

"I have been reminded of your sincere faith, which first lived in your grandmother . . . and in your mother" (2 Timothy 1:5).

A pastor who was observing the 50th anniversary of his ordination was asked what he considered the primary calling of the ministry. Without hesitation he replied, "It is to present Jesus Christ so that people come to know and love him and give evidence of this commitment."

Eunice and her mother placed high priority on their son and grandson, Timothy, coming to faith in Christ. Bible scholars believe Timothy's father was Greek and probably not a Christian. But Timothy's mother and grandmother made up for that lack by teaching him and praying for him until the faith that lived in them lived in him too.

As Christian mothers, have we made this our primary goal? What are we doing to encourage our children to give their hearts and lives to Jesus? Does the way we live tell them that this is what we desire most for them?

It is important to ask ourselves these questions, for at the end of life, if not before, we, like the pastor, will discover that this is our highest calling as mothers.

O Christ, I do want my children to belong to you. Be at work in their hearts to draw them to you.

Talk to your children about their relationship to Jesus.

Playing God

"Cast all your anxiety on him because he cares for you" (1 Peter 5:7).

I picked up the phone. My friend, the pastor of a large church, was chuckling. "Got caught today," he said, "Doc nailed me good."

"What do you mean?" I asked puzzled.

"I went for my checkup for blood pressure," he began. "Been having trouble with it going up. Doc checked it, wound up the black arm wrap and wrote something down on my chart. Then he peered at me over his half-glasses. 'What you need,' he said, 'is a little humility.'

"All the way home from his office I pondered this statement. Then I began to smile to myself. Doc has known me for twenty years. When he said I needed a little humility, he was telling me to stop playing God, to learn that the burdens and problems of my people only God can bear."

My friend chuckled again. "Funny, isn't it, that a preacher needs to be told that by a doctor?"

> *Loving God, I confess that as a mother I too sometimes*
> *try to play God. Forgive me. Increase my faith. Teach*
> *me to cast all my burdens on you.*

When do you play God? Can you relinquish this now and let God be God? Talk to him about this.

How Big Is Your World?

"For Macedonia and Achaia have been pleased to make a contribution for the poor among the saints in Jerusalem" (Romans 15:26).

A television program about the woods of eastern Canada showed large numbers of moose living in the lowland coniferous forests. "The area is dotted with numerous shallow lakes that supply the moose with ample pondweed and water lilies," the narrator commented. "Together with grass and sedges, the twigs of birch and aspen, and the varied diet. So content are the moose that most of them live out their lives within a 10-mile radius."

One of our sons spent a year in East Africa, where people struggle to eke out a survival. When he returned to the United States, he tried to share what he had seen, but many only drew together their eyebrows when he talked.

After the TV program about the moose, our son said quietly, "Lots of people are like moose, aren't they? They are so contented because all their needs and most of their wants are satisfied that they never move beyond a 10-mile radius in their compassion and concern for other. And then there are others who may never travel farther than a hundred miles from their homes, but who encircle the people of the world with their love and concern."

Help me enlarge my circle of love, O Lord.

What can you do to give your children a world vision?

In Mother's Face

"I have great confidence in you; I take great pride in you. I am greatly encouraged" (2 Corinthians 7:4).

Robert Louis Stevenson's road to success was slow and pain-filled. Because of ill health, he abandoned studies in engineering and earned a degree in law instead. But he wasn't happy practicing law. So he began to do what he wanted to all the time—write—even though his father frowned.

The ill health he had known earlier continued to frustrate him. In search of relief he traveled to France, England, America, and Switzerland, and finally found a degree of relief in the Samoan islands. But living there meant being deprived of close association of his family. Stevenson and his father had become reconciled, but it was his mother who Stevenson missed most.

On a short visit to Scotland he sat one day in his parents' home leafing through a scrapbook his mother had put together with newspaper clippings and reviews about him. A friend who had dropped by to greet him, sat watching.

"Is fame all it's cracked up to be?" the friend asked.

Stevenson was silent for a moment. Then, "Yes," he said. "Yes, it is when I see my mother's face."

> Gracious God, help me to live in such a way that I shall bring joy, pride, and encouragement to those who love me most.

When have you been proud of your children? Have you told them? Does your face reveal your pride and joy in them?

Pilgrim Spirits

"The Lord watches over the alien" (Psalm 146:9).

Eleven times we have moved in our married life. "You never stay in one place long enough to put down roots," a friend said one day. "Do we have to put down roots?" I asked.

As I read the Scriptures, I find God's people quite often on the move. Abraham went from Mesopotamia to Haran to Canaan. Joseph found himself in Egypt, and eventually his father and brothers joined him there. Then the children of Israel moved to their promised land.

The symbol of rootedness comes from trees, and is a helpful one. But we human beings are much more adaptable to new environments than trees are. We stand at the top of God's created order. We have the ability not only to survive, but to grow even in a mobile lifestyle—that is if our roots are in God.

It is important for us to understand this for we are a mobile society, with the average family moving once every few years. True, losses and regrets accompany each move, but we should also keep our eyes open to the new opportunities that are provided. Being a pilgrim can remind us more clearly of the fact that we need to depend on God to give us a feeling of security in our changing world.

> Help us remember, O God, that here we have no abiding city. Give us pilgrim spirits to find our permanent dwelling in you.

In what ways can mobility be an opportunity for spiritual and personal growth?

When God Is Silent

"O God, do not keep silent; be not quiet, O God, be not still" (Psalm 83:1).

The orchestral movement ended abruptly. The violinists tucked their violins under their arms. The horn players rested their horns on their knees. The cellists lowered their bows. Still, the conductor kept marking out the beat with his baton. Then, after some full minutes of silence, the violinists placed their instruments under their chins, and their bows drew out sweet music. Soon the other instruments joined in a triumphant, soaring crescendo of praise and exaltation, and I realized that the moments of silence were a deliberate and planned, though unexpected, part of the movement.

Are there times in your life when you cry out to God and only silence greets you? Do not despair. The wise Conductor is still marking out the beat. Times when God seems silent can be opportunities for us to pray, reflect, and grow. When the sense of God's presence returns, our exhilaration will be all the greater.

> Grant me grace, O God, to grow in those times when you seem so distant. Help me remember that your Spirit is always as close as the very air I breathe, even when I do not sense your presence.

Spend some time praising God, even if it appears that he is silent.

Blended Family

"The Spirit himself testifies with our Spirit that we are God's children" (Romans 8:16).

Jason is eight years old and is getting acquainted with some new family members. His mother and father were divorced four years ago, and his mother recently remarried.

Jason likes his new father, and also his two new sisters. Most of the time he thinks it's fun to have sisters, though there are times when he misses having his mother all to himself. And there were other adjustments that had to be made, too, like having to share everything from the TV to desserts after supper.

A blended family brings adjustments for parents, too. There are new routines to get used to, conflicts to iron out, old memories to work through. Sometimes the children of one parent feel that preferential treatment is being shown to the others. But along with the challenges comes a chance to get to know and love new family members—to extend the circle of God's love within the family.

> *Dear God, help me to welcome others as brothers and sisters in Christ.*

If you have a blended family, what have been some of the biggest trouble spots for you? The biggest joys?

Think About Such Things

". . . think about such things. . . . And the God of peace will be with you" (Philippians 4:8-9).

Paul advises us to think about whatever is:
> *true*, that which can be relied on;
> *noble*, that which has the dignity of holiness about it;
> *right*, that which acknowledges God as the giver of all and honors him;
> *pure*, that which is so clean that it can be brought into the presence of God and pass his scrutiny;
> *lovely*, that which calls forth love from us;
> *admirable*, that which we would be happy to think about in the presence of God;
> *excellent*, the highest, most noble;
> *praiseworthy*, those thoughts for which God could commend us.

Think on these things, Paul said, and he promises us the result: "the God of peace will be with you."

> *Help me bring my thought life under your lordship, God.*

How do the television programs and movies you watch fit Paul's criteria?

What People Need Most

"His mother said to the servants, 'Do whatever he tells you' " (John 2:5).

What extraordinary faith and confidence Mary had in her son! Did this attitude of trust and expectation characterize the home atmosphere in which Jesus grew up? Did Mary constantly encourage, believe in, and challenge Jesus? Did she see him, in response, doing things at home that made her marvel? Was this why she turned to him now?

In one of her books, Adela Rogers St. Johns recalls standing one late afternoon on a balcony of the Ambassador Hotel in Los Angeles with the noted wit and playwright Wilson Mizner. "As we watched the steady stream of traffic go out Wilshire Boulevard," she writes, "Mizner said, 'I wonder how many of these men and women are going home to somebody who believes in them and cheers for them. That's what people need most.' "

Mary believed in Jesus, and Jesus responded to her faith in him.

Lord, may the words with which we greet each other at the end of the day be words of affirmation.

Are those whose lives you touch becoming more confident and able because of your expressed faith in what God can do in and through them?

Growth Through Conflict

"I plead . . . agree with each other in the Lord" (Philippians 4:2).

I had looked forward to having all our children home this summer. It probably will be the last time all of us will be together. We've had some beautiful times together, but," and the mother sighed, "we've had some explosions too. I've felt like such a failure! Why do we have to fight?"

Conflict. Why do we have it?

One contributing factor surely has been the increase in education. Years ago when fewer people were educated, more people responded without protest to authority in government, church, and home. Today, as people are becoming better informed, they are daring to question.

This is good from a biblical point of view. The Bible underscores again and again the worth of the individual. The Bible deplores the domination of people by a small powerful group. God wants all his children to grow up and mature. Growing up will include clarifying our own positions, adopting certain values as our own, and coming to a faith in God that is personally ours. This process will often produce conflict. So when you hear conflict in your family, instead of feeling like a parent who has failed, rejoice that growth is taking place.

O Holy Spirit, when I see the blossoms of childhood dropping, help me to have faith to believe they will be replaced by the fruit of maturity.

What were some of the struggles and tensions you faced during your adolescence?

What Do You Have in Your Hand?

"The Lord said to him, 'What is that in your hand?' "
(Exodus 4:2).

God had a job for Moses to do. He wanted him to lead the children of Israel out of bondage to independence. "I can't do it," Moses said. "I'm no orator. I'd never be able to persuade the people."

Moses thought of the gifts he didn't have and felt inadequate and frustrates. In response, God simply asked another question, "What do you have in your hand?"

Moses stared at the stick in his hand and wondered what God meant. Yet God used that stick in an extraordinary way to accomplish the miracles that plagued Egypt until the Pharaoh let the Israelites go. Moses' eloquent rhetoric wasn't needed after all. All that was needed was his obedience and his willingness to use what he had in his hand.

Often we feel we would be better wives and mothers if only—and we name all the things we lack. God says to us too, "What do you have in your hand? What are the gifts and abilities I have given you? Use them, walk in obedience, and trust me for all the rest."

> O my God, you are the spring, I am the brook.
> Because of this refreshing waters can flow from my life.
> Thank you.

Make a list of the gifts and abilities God has given you.

Holding On and Letting Go

"Trust in God; trust also in me" (John 14:1).

Holding on and letting go. Mothers live with these tensions.

Moses' mother held on in faith that God would save her child. She had to let him go when she placed him in a cradle on the riverbank. She held on to him as she nursed him and recited to him in story the history of his people. She had to let him go when Pharaoh's daughter claimed him.

Hannah held out in tenacious faith that God would give her a child. She had to let him go when she sent him off to be raised in the temple by the aged Eli.

The tensions of holding on and letting go always will be there. Sooner or later our children will leave home. A poignant sorrow that the old must pass, that nothing will ever be the same again may steal into our hearts. But a slow awakening peace can replace the sadness as we realize that only as we let go can growth take place. Wise are the parents who have been able to gradually release their hold on their children while they have still been at home and who have introduced means by which the children's perceptions can widen. Then the children will be better able to listen, evaluate, judge, and make wise choices.

> Dear God, you have blessed us with children. Enable us to teach them whatever is just and good. Give us grace to let them go even as we hold on in faith for them.

In what respects is it difficult for you to let go?

The Song of a Humble, Thankful Heart

Based on Psalm 139

O Lord, I am not puffed up with pride.
I have not fantasized myself into believing
I am someone that I am not.
But I have seen myself as you have made me.
I am at rest in you.
Even as a child, asleep in my arms, is at rest,
so I am at rest in you.
For you made me as I am.
I praise you as I consider my uniqueness.
What a good job you did!
You know me through and through.
You have always known me,
from the time I was a baby until now.
You rejoiced in me while I was yet
a developing fetus in my mother's uterus.
Even then you began to plan surprises for me.
How meticulous your care is of me!
Awake or asleep, I am with you.
The Lord will fulfill his purpose for me.
Your steadfast love, O Lord, endures forever.
Do not forsake the work of your hand.

A Plea for Wisdom Not to Be Deceived

Based on Psalm 12

Help, Lord, for violence has seized our world.
People think nothing of deception,
whether through word, ads, or political jargon.
They speak with flattering lips and double hearts.
Because the poor are taken advantage of,
because the needy moan,
"I will now arise," says the Lord.
"I will begin to work on behalf of the poor."
The promises of the Lord are not like
the deceptive words of the greedy.
The promises of the Lord are trustworthy,
tested and tried thousands of times
by his people in troubled times.
O Lord, save us from being caught up
and swept away by this generation.
But I am not guiltless, O God,
if my life revolves around myself, my family,
and the things I want;
if my eyes do not see the needy
and my ears do not hear their cry;
if my heart does not want to learn of their need
lest I feel uncomfortable in my comfort.
Arouse me, O God. Open my eyes
and save me from being deceived.

A Prayer of Confession

Based on Psalm 37

Fret not because of the prosperity
of your friends and relatives.
Do not envy them.
For they may succeed and flourish in this life,
but if their hearts are not given to God,
what will their prosperity and success mean
in the life to come?
God orders our steps
and though we sin and fall
and become weary and discouraged
in our struggle against sin,
God lifts us up and restores us.
Trust in the Lord.
Do good and follow God.
Yes, follow the one who, though rich,
became poor for your sake.
In this way you offer to him a sacrifice
of love and loyalty, and
joy and peace will live in you again.

An Appeal for Forgiveness and Renewal

Based on Psalm 18

I love you, O God, my strength.
You are my friend,
who encourages me to keep on believing,
my Savior, who knows what to say
to lift me out of despair,
the one to whom I can pour out
all the concerns of my heart,
and who reminds me that you are always with me
to pick me up and set me on my way again.
Discouragement and frustration were overcoming me,
irritation and anger were sweeping over me.
In my distress I called on the Lord.
To my God I cried for help.
He heard my voice,
and my cries reached his ears.
I am sorry, Lord, that so often
I fall short of what you want me to be.
Forgive me. Cleanse me. Renew me.
I thank the Lord that he has heard me.
God has declared forgiveness to me
and assured me of unfailing love and faithfulness.
I will arise, forgiven.
My God understands
and will surely help me.

A Prayer for Wisdom

Based on Psalm 1

Truly happy are those
who do not get carried away by current trends
or believe deceptive merchandising slogans
but who find contentment in simple gifts
and make the Word of God their guide
day and night.
They are like the creosote bush,
whose taproot draws nourishment
from deep underneath the parched desert floor,
staying fresh and sound.
But those who follow the trends of this age
are like the fluff of dandelions,
which the wind blows away.
Those who turn their backs on God
and practice self-centeredness
will lose out in the end.
But happy are those
who take their direction from God,
who know that everything they have
is a gift God has given
to be shared with those in need.

A Cry for Faith Among Family

Based on Psalm 39

O Lord, I have told my family
the glad news of your deliverance.
I have not been silent, as you know,
I have not hidden your promise of salvation,
but have spoken openly of your faithfulness.
Do not, O Lord, withhold your mercy from me.
Let your steadfast love and faithfulness
keep me believing and deliver me
from my anxieties.
Turn the hearts of my family
so that they will no longer simply
smile at me tolerantly when I speak of you.
I said, "I will guard my tongue;
I will not nag at my family."
I have held my peace, but to no avail.
My distress mounts again.
I long to bring them back to you,
but I cannot.
Hear my prayer, O Lord, and give ear to my cry.
Do not be untouched by my tears.
Make haste to answer me, O Lord,
my rock and my salvation.

The Prayer of a Trusting Heart

Based on Psalm 27

The Lord has shown faithfulness to me.
Is there anything I should fear?
The Lord is the staying power of my life.
Is there anything of which I should be afraid?
When anxieties about my parents and their future
threaten to choke me,
I will turn to the Lord.
If my health deteriorates,
and there is nothing I can do,
even then I will not forget to trust in God.
I am confident, O Lord,
that you will not forsake us
in the day of trouble.
You will protect us and save us
and lift us out of despair
if only we turn to you.
Teach me your will, O God,
and lead me clearly
when perplexities and uncertainties trouble me.
For in you,
my mighty and powerful God,
do I trust.

A Prayer of Thanksgiving

Based on Ephesians 1:3-14

Almighty and eternal God,
hidden from my sight,
I marvel that you have chosen
to breathe your Spirit into me,
that you have inclined my mind to seek you
and my heart to love you.
O Lord, I praise and magnify your name
that you have chosen me as your own,
that you have adopted me
as one of your very own children,
with a right to the inheritance
you keep in trust for me.
I thank you that you have
placed your hand on my shoulder,
that you want me no matter how often
I falter or fall or mess things up.
You still want me,
and you are prepared
to pick me up and carry me
when life becomes too much for me.
O God, my Savior,
I praise and worship you.

A Prayer for Strength

Based on 1 Corinthians 9:24-27

Almighty God, give me a brave and trusting heart
as I begin my work today.
Only through effort and pain
can I walk the upward way.
Be my fellow traveler and walk with me.
Enable me to face what you send
or allow to come
with the strength you supply.
When you grant success to my efforts,
don't let me forget to dwell in your Word
and live in obedience to it.
When you call me to go through the dark valley,
let me not persuade myself that I know a way around.
Let me not refuse any opportunity of service
that I can fulfill today.
Rescue me from any temptation
that may be lying in wait for me.
O God, give me the grace I need today
to be one of your people,
a child of God.

A Prayer for My Children

Based on Psalm 34

I remember the many times
I have sought the Lord.
He has answered me
and delivered me from my fears.
I am glad I can believe
that the angel of the Lord
watches over my family
and will keep them.
For those who fear the Lord will not lack
any of the most precious things
life can offer us.
"Come, my children, listen to me.
I will teach you the fear of the Lord.
Keep your heart from covetousness,
and your life free from
the worship of things.
Turn your back on self-centeredness.
Seek the good of others.
Pursue faithfulness to your God."
I do trust you, God.
Let your steadfast love draw my children to you
even as I put my trust in you.

The Prayer of a Working Mother

All day long I mourned and grieved,
for tomorrow is the day I must leave my child
in the care of another.
My little one knows it not,
but I do, and wonder,
what will she think tomorrow
when I drop her off
and don't come back in an hour or two to pick her up?
Does she understand time?
Does she know how long
four, five, even six hours is?
Will she grow anxious, restless, miss me, cry?
Or, as the days pass, learn to love another
more than me?
Will she care when finally, at night, weary
I return
to hold her close, to stroke her hair,
to bury my nose in her neck,
to love her and love her and love her?
O God, how happy I am to be a mother.
But oh, how it hurts tonight!
Hear my cry, O Lord.
Bind up the wounds of my heart.
Ease my pain, dry my tears,
help me to lean on you.
And cradle our little one in your strong arms,
that she may feel loved and secure.

The Prayer of an Aging Mother

Lord, what once I could have done
with youthful vigor
I can no longer do.
But grant me, now older,
wiser insight,
a humbler heart,
gentleness and love.
Then shall I be able to live in harmony
with all my kin.
Then shall I love well and wisely,
feel one with them.
Then shall I be truly yours and theirs,
your life, my life within.
O live, O love through me
till what my loved ones see in me
reflects your beauty, patience, purity.

The Prayer of a Grieving Mother

Death saves; does not destroy.
When I awake from death's long sleep
my daughter, my son,
with arms outstretched I'll welcome.
Tenfold more mine they will once again become,
my girl and boy.
To these now-empty arms my brood shall run,
and I, with them, to those
from whose my earthly history began.

Bible Readings Series